AN INTRODUCTION TO PSYCHOANALYTIC RESEARCH

Kenneth Mark Colby

AN

Introduction

TO

Psychoanalytic

Research

BASIC BOOKS, INC. · NEW YORK

To Erin and Peter
Fin de Soledad

Preface

Psychoanalysis is a branch of science. It proposes a system of theory and observations about human behavior. The training of psychoanalysts has been limited for the most part to the transmission of this system without encouragement of original work.

But the coming generation of psychoanalysts is interested in discovery of new facts and concepts. Unsolved problems will require the application of scientific methods appropriate to psychoanalytic data by those trained in psychoanalytic theory and observation. To aid the beginning investigator in his first searchings in this difficult field, the following Introduction has been prepared.

Kenneth Mark Colby

Ross, California
July 1960

Contents

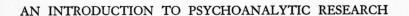

AN INTRODUCTION TO PSYCHOANALYTIC RESEARCH

:I:
Scientific Investigation

PURE AND APPLIED SCIENCE

Textbooks, those stolid arbiters, draw distinctions between pure science, applied science, and practical art. In pure science we study natural phenomena, in applied science we attempt to produce a change in these phenomena. Practical art consists of skills employed in exertions to produce the desired change.

If pressed, one can describe parallel distinctions in psychoanalysis. We study persons as they are, we attempt to change aspects of their behavior, and we utilize practical skills in bringing about changes. These distinctions do not as yet represent divisions of labor among psychoanalysts. And they are only useful literary devices for descriptions of general science. But we can use them to discuss research in the psychoanalytic situation.

[3]

An Introduction to Psychoanalytic Research

In modern psychoanalysis we are trying to develop scientific methods appropriate to our data and problems. Our systematic data consist of observations made in the psychoanalytic situation, and our problems concern a consistent theory of human behavior. To discover new knowledge we strive to augment both pure and applied scientific efforts.

Our efforts meet various receptions depending on connotations of the term "scientific." Scholars and artists use the term pejoratively to abhor, whereas physicists use it eulogistically to dignify. From some quarters there emanates a steady prating about what is and what is not science and who qualifies for the honor. Certain psychologists, with the quaint conceit of self-congratulation, have declared that psychoanalysis is not a science.[1] *

Rather than waste time replying to seedy tirades about our scientific status, psychoanalytic investigators should simply work diligently to discover knowledge useful for our field and allow the results to speak for themselves. We utilize approaches to our subject matter which can be exalted by the label "scientific" whether self-appointed custodians of the term agree or do not. Indeed, the loudest of them has been shown to be opaque regarding the essential nature of scientific activity.[2]

A WORKING DEFINITION

It seems agreed in broad terms that science constitutes a human quest for knowledge about natural phenomena. We

* Notes will be found at the end of each chapter.

[4]

increase this knowledge by searching for and finding useful generalizations. Instead of trying to define science further in the abstract, let us describe what the scientist, as a scientist, does.

A scientist is a person who makes observations and/or experiments to obtain data relevant to a hypothesis about a problem in a selected portion of the world of experience in order to decide whether or not the hypothesis is correct.

Each important term in this description will be discussed briefly.

Person. A scientist is first a person subject to the psychodynamic laws of motivation. It is caricature to exclude his passions, commitments, urges, and dreams. The life-histories of scientists,[3] reveal interesting regularities, and some arresting clinical observations have been made about them.[4] There is no need to remind analysts that, in investigating persons, there are advantages to being a person, since it is experiences with others which are the most consequential of natural phenomena in human life.

Observations and/or Experiments. To describe and distinguish these will require some time, so I will devote the next chapter to them.

Data. A scientist takes the observations he makes on phenomena and converts them into data which are (*a*) objective, *i.e.,* intersubjectively confirmable, (*b*) significant for a theory, (*c*) measurable, (*d*) generalizable. Generalizable means that in science we are interested in single phenomena as they instance a general class. We search for useful *generalizations* which extend beyond particular data.

Hypothesis. A hypothesis represents a bright idea, a hunch solution, an intuitive guess about a problem. A good hypothesis suggests decidable questions which, when answered, solve the problem. Intuition, a product of unconscious computations and operations, is underplayed only by the methodolatrous in science; great scientists respect its role.[5] To formulate a good hypothesis as a tentative solution to a problem requires ingenuity, inventiveness, and creativeness—virtues about which we know so little that we resignedly call them gifts (from whom?), mysterious and unteachable.

Problem. A scientist usually initiates an inquiry because he becomes gripped by a problem. It is the nature of the problem that determines the nature of the scientific methods to be used. The methods chosen must be appropriate not only to the problem but also to the stage of inquiry. Scientific methods in early descriptive and exploratory stages are different from methods required in later, rigorous confirmatory stages. Einstein remarked that a precise formulation of a problem is more essential than its solution. Another gift of the eminent scientist is that he can see how the solution to this particular problem has a bearing on other problems. That a scientist senses a problem exists in a subject matter of course means that he experiences some dissatisfaction with the status quo. The currently accepted answers to problems in his field are not acceptable to him. He seeks new answers and even finds new problems hitherto unrecognized.

Selected Portion. No one but a scholastic dares attempt solutions to all the problems of human experience. From the history of science in the past four hundred years we know that a search for knowledge in the form of reliable generalizations is most fruitful when we focus on specific, isolable portions of experience in the world. The problems of selected, delimitable areas are thus rendered manageable and we can proceed, a step at a time, toward useful knowledge.

Decide. Decisions in science require the weighing of evidence. Such judgments utilize quantitative measures, the matching of congruences, and other mathematical aids.

Correct. Whether or not a hypothesis is correct means, "Does this hunch idea in my mind about a problem in external reality correspond to what actually can be found out there in external reality?" If the intramind hypothesis about reality is correct, it should be confirmable by observation of the external world. If it is correct, *how* correct is it? That is, how much confidence can we have in it within certain limits and are we willing to act on it?

This sketch of a scientist *qua* scientist serves as an elementary description of scientific activity. It does not answer the question "What is science?" for that, after all, is not a scientific question. But as an initial definition it will at least guide us through a consideration of scientific investigation in psychoanalysis.

SOME HISTORY

A working investigator need have little knowledge of the philosophy or even the history of science. But I would like to introduce some historical remarks at this point because they are relevant to an understanding of our present position and our scientific needs in modern psychoanalysis. Psychoanalysis is still mainly in a descriptive, natural history stage, and we can compare it historically to other fields which have advanced to explanatory stages. Such comparisons may help us find suitable ways to advance.

Most historians date the rise of modern science from around 1600. Before that time, of course, there were attempts deserving an honorific use of the term "scientific." Egyptians and Babylonians were systematically interested in movements of the planets (early physics), in plants and animals (early biology), in diseases and wounds (early medicine), in cooking, dyeing and metallurgy (early chemistry), and in counting, measuring, land surveying, calendar-making (early mathematics).

Then, as always happens in history books, came the Greeks. Except for a small school of empiricists, they were not much in favor of making observations and experiments, apparently feeling these were degrading manual tasks best left to slaves. Pythagoras did pluck stretched strings and show that the pitch depended on the length of string allowed to vibrate, and of course Archimedes conducted many experiments. But the main contribution of the Greeks lay in deductive geometry and in the deductive method. By "deductive method" we mean that, given a premise, certain conclusions can be derived from it purely by a process of inference. Syllogisms are well-known illustrations of deductive method. For instance: all psychoanalysts are rich, Ralph is a psychoanalyst, therefore, Ralph . . . and so forth.

Euclid's *Elements* represents the best example of Greek deductive geometry and deductive method.

But where would the initial premise come from? How do we know that all psychoanalysts are rich? The Greeks answered that the initial premise was self-evident or given by intuition. Out of this confidence in pure intuition developed rationalism, the belief that man could solve problems and increase his knowledge through intuition and deduction alone.[6]

Scientific inquiry represents a search for useful generalizations. A scientist would like to be able to say that some implication holds for all things of a specified kind. If one can then incorporate an individual fact into a generalization, one can make a prediction with some degree of certainty. The Greeks—for example, Plato—believed there were two entities in the world—physical things and ideas. Aware of the unreliability of sense observation, they turned to ideas as superior to things in their truth value and having a higher reality. Therefore, to arrive at generalizations of the highest certainty one should examine ideas rather than things. What added confidence to this belief was that it worked so well in geometry. But this search for certainty led to an anti-empirical attitude and rationalism. The Greeks turned away from observation to reason. They made advances in mathematics but, prejudiced against empirical methods, they could not get beyond the limitations of intuited premises and deduction.

And the Romans did not help much either. They were certainly interested in things more than in ideas, but they wanted immediately to do something with things rather than to understand them. Their stamp of mind favored applied technologies rather than pure science. They were businessmen, lawyers, soldiers, and administrators, much like the power elite of contemporary Americans. They applied scientific ideas of the Greeks to problems but did not replenish the source with new ideas discovered through pure science investigation. Later these constrictions were tightened further by Christianity, leading to a dark interlude for science. It was left to the Arabs to carry on and add to scientific knowledge. They introduced the decimal system (and by the way, Omar Khayyám was the leading Arab astronomer and mathematician of his time).

In thirteenth-century Europe there occurred a rediscovery of Arab science and of the few Greek empiricists such as Democritus (not the orator, but the atomist). The fall of Constantinople to the Turks brought a flow of scholarly emigrés who had preserved Greek empirical knowledge and who now introduced it into Europe. In contrast to rationalism, empiricism consisted of the view that sense observation was the primary source and ultimate judge of knowledge. Scholastic philosophy, a system of belief about God, man, and the world, had been the final product of Greek rationalism compounded with Christianity. But now it was challenged by empiricists who found a way of combining rational and empirical approaches to knowledge to produce a much greater yield. Modern science began around 1600 with this combined approach of observation plus reasoning. Observations were used for knowledge of the present and past while reasoning could be used for predictions of the future.

THE SCIENTIFIC REVOLUTION

Combining rationalism and empiricism, deductive and inductive methods, scientists now began to make great advances in the search for dependable generalizations. It is rightly called a scientific revolution, and it took place chiefly in mechanics, the science of motion. Celestial and terrestrial mechanics spurted ahead with the work of Copernicus, Kepler, Galileo, and Newton. Physics bounded in front of other sciences, and it is still the most successful branch of science. But not only because it had a head start.

Why did the revolution take place in mechanics and why is it still the area of the most reliable generalizations? There are five groups of answers.

1. Problems of motion had been worked on by great and average minds for two thousand years. A scientist describes what he observes, describes regularities in what he observes, and describes systematic attempts to effect predictable regularities. In two thousand years there was time for thousands of observations to be made and for regularities to be discovered (fortunately, they were there to discover). Also during that long a span there was plenty of time to correct errors in the observations and to revise concepts. It takes time, even when great minds are at work, to close in on a problem. Science moves slowly and gropingly toward successively better approximations. Psychoanalysts should not

feel too discouraged with their results to date. They have been working only sixty years in a new area—and against strong human opposition to exploration of that area.

2. Observations in mechanical physics are simple to make. Observations of planets and of falling bodies can be made by an ordinary man without the special knowledge or experience of an expert.

3. Experiments are easily managed. An experiment is distinguished from simple observation and measurement in that it involves a deliberate isolation and manipulation of factors in an artificially simplified situation. Although planets cannot be manipulated, all sorts of terrestrial motion can be experimented with. Ease of observation and experiment in turn mean an easy access to sources of data.

4. The problems of mechanics are suitable for mathematical treatment. One might wonder why the revolutionary breakthrough did not occur in chemistry, since, there, laboratory experiments are the easiest to carry out. But alchemy and chemistry did not advance very far because they lacked powerful quantitative, mathematical explanations. Galileo showed that we can ignore properties of taste, smell, or color of bodies in motion and confine our attention to properties capable of quantitative measurement and calculation such as time, distance and weight.

5. Finally, the physical world is quite simple compared to the biological world. The physical world is loosely coupled in that one can dissect it and study it a piece at a time to find regularities. Also, processes in the physical world are continuous, allowing us to write simple linear equations for

mathematical description. And lastly, the physical world is relatively stable, allowing us to exert effects on one part of it without producing a general chaos in all its parts.

All of these characteristics made the physical world a most likely area for the breakthrough of the scientific revolution. Notice that none of the five characteristics holds for the world of persons. In the domain of persons, we are still struggling to find the crucial regularities upon which depend other scientific steps toward explanation.

The strength of the scientific revolution in physics lay in the combination of observation, experiment, measurement, and mathematical formulation. Physics eventually was able to discover relations, not so much between phenomena as between suitable concepts in which phenomena could be expressed. In its mathematical formulae we find the contribution of rationalism in which future observed facts are deducible by reason alone. It was mainly from physics that we inherited the ideal model of current science, consisting of observations plus mathematical explanation plus derivations from mathematical explanation leading to implications tested by observation.

This cycle of observation–deduction–observation has enabled physics to formulate the most powerful generalizations in science. By powerful I mean that a very large number of factual consequences can be deduced from a single generalization. In classical physics this is exemplified by the generalizations of Isaac Newton. Think of the enormous number of facts which can be deduced from his Third Law.

Thus far the ideal procedural model has been powerful

and successful in physics. The method itself developed historically step-by-step through successive transformations of human viewpoints toward science, and it is not yet a finished product. What will the next transformation be? For the physics model has limitations in biological science, and especially in behavioral science. We will have to make another transformation in scientific method and develop new approaches more appropriate to our problems and to our subject matter. As already emphasized, in science the subject matter determines the method, not vice versa. However, since we do not as yet have the new transformation we should try to exhaust the possibilities of the current procedural model. As yet we cannot say it has failed in psychoanalysis because it has not even been given a fair try. If we can find ways of applying it to our problems we must do so, for it has proved its worth as a successful way of increasing knowledge.

After the scientific revolution in physics came revolutions in chemistry and medicine. Until Harvey, medicine as a science had been limited to descriptive anatomy. But Harvey utilized the procedural model of physics in demonstrating that the blood circulated. The invention of the air pump had led him to wonder if the heart might be a pump. But more important than this simple analogy was his combination of observation, experiment, and quantitative formulation. He deduced that if the heart pumps two ounces at each beat and beats sixty-five times per minute, in a few hours it would pump more blood than the body contained; therefore the blood must circulate. Since there were no microscopes at that time, Harvey further inferred the existence of capillary connections between arteries and veins. Their eventual discovery served as an observational confirmation of his inference.[7]

THE BOGY OF MATHEMATICS

Several times in this historical account I have spoken of mathematics. Mathematics is a forbidding subject to most psychoanalysts. They immediately (and groaningly) think of the complications of trigonometry or differential calculus and doubt if these could ever be suitably used in solving problems of human behavior. There are two sorts of extremists: those awed by the quantitative feel that only if you can measure something is it important, whereas others are convinced that, if you can measure it, it is not important. Many psychoanalysts belong to the latter faction. They have witnessed the frequent misuse of numbers in academic psychology and they well know the ridiculous pseudo-rigor of those who count irrelevant entities simply to report that something has been counted. But I would like to encourage a fresh look at quantitation and mathematics. If we aspire to the ermine of science we must reconsider the aids of mathematics in our field.

Mathematics is a special language, but it is a language with many dialects. What do we mean by a mathematical formulation? The first step is to assign a number, a letter, or some other symbol to an observation. This is the most elementary, but nonetheless powerful, mathematical operation. We make the qualitative decision to observe some property or attribute and then count how many things possess this attribute. All things having the attribute are said to belong to a specific class. We count the things in this specific class and represent the count by a number. Such is the basis of all statistics. Once quantities have been established, the next step is to relate the quantities according to certain rules or formulae.

In psychoanalytic research there has been a general reluctance to count and a mistrust of numbers. Perhaps one reason why Mendel's work in genetics was ignored for thirty years was that his contemporaries considered it mere numerology; he counted percentages. Lysenkoists even today resist the use of numbers in genetics. But to count is extremely useful and necessary. It is the basis of almost all other mathematical methods used in science.[8] In modern psychoanalysis we make use of probability theory based on relative frequencies obtained by simple counting.

The Greeks developed deductive geometry to a high level. They also laid foundations for the theory of numbers. Numbers and geometry were important for astronomy and for mechanical physics in general. With the scientific revolution of the Renaissance, came new mathematical methods. Descartes invented analytic geometry, which linked the numerical geometry of the ancients with new developments in algebra. Newton and Leibniz invented the calculus to deal with problems of motion, in particular a change of motion in magnitude or direction. In science these mathematical aids offered a basic advantage in that, after assigning symbols to observations, one could then manipulate the symbols according to certain rules and arrive at new information about observations. To manipulate symbols, rather than things or observations of things in the external world, saves time and effort.

Arithmetic, algebra, geometry, and calculus proved to be indispensable for physics. Other branches of mathematics are more suitable for the problems of psychoanalysis, as we shall see in a later chapter. Probability theory, nonparametric statistics, set theory, and new forms of algebra are applicable to our problems. Just as Newton and Leibniz invented a new mathematical tool suitable for the change of motion problem, we will have to invent new mathematical tools to deal with specific problems in human behavior. One area of new research in psychoanalysis will consist of inventing mathematical aids that will bring us the time and labor-saving device of manipulating symbols instead of observations and provide us with mathematical formulae from which new deducible consequences can be observed.

TWENTIETH CENTURY VIEWPOINTS

Let us come now to the present and consider some recent views of importance for psychoanalytic investigation.

Certainty. It is now felt by scientists that the human desire and quest for certainty is futile. We cannot state generalizations of the type *if A, then always B*. We are limited to saying *if A, then probably B or B in some regular percentage of cases*. Induction—i.e., inferring from the particular to the general—cannot *logically* be justified. To say that induction has thus far worked, and is therefore justified is itself an inductive inference. All knowledge is probable knowledge within certain limits, and the justification of induction is practical only in that it is the best course of action known to us thus far.

Nor is deduction entirely certain. For Goedel [9] has demonstrated that deductive method contains inherent limitations of incompleteness and that it is theoretically impossible to prove the internal consistency of deductive systems. With both inductive and deductive methods open to so many questions one might consider our search for precise knowledge a chimera. Although we cannot attain *certain* knowledge, we can strive for demonstrably *useful* knowledge of great help in the choice of human actions.

Science does not definitively solve problems once and for all. It proceeds through successively better approximations, stumbling from one series of mistakes to another. Physics has proceeded from the approximations of Aristotle to the approximations of Newton to the approximations of Einstein. And Einstein did not have the last word to say. Today physicists state there are two unsatisfactory areas in their field: relativity theory and quantum theory.

Degrees of uncertainty in all sense observation, experiment, and reasoning require that we familiarize ourselves with probability theory. Later I will take up probability theory and its relevance for psychoanalytic investigation.

Relativity Theory. Einstein's demonstration that observations and hence concepts depend on the position and state of motion of observers has had a compelling effect on all scientific thinking. It destroyed absolutes in our world picture and mathematically alerted us to the observer-observed interaction.

Language. Logic and philosophy have made important contributions to knowledge of how language operates in human and scientific thought. There has been a useful clarification of the relations between words and their referents—that is, the things they denote. An important distinction has been made between a statement of truth and a definition. Scientific definitions must be read from right to left instead of left to right. For example, when I say, "Two rods in different places *are* equal," I really mean, "Equal is what we will agree to *call* two rods in different places." In psychoanalysis, when we *define* the superego, saying, "The superego is the precipitate of abandoned object-cathexes of the Oedipus situation," we do not mean, as a statement of truth about reality, this *is* the superego. We only mean, "Let us *call* the precipitate of abandoned object-cathexes of the Oedipus situation, the superego."

From logic also has come the testability theory of meaning, which requires that a statement be considered scientifically (not psychologically) meaningful only if it can be verified as true or false in principle. Questions such as "What is the cause of the universe?" "What is the purpose of life?" "How did matter come from nothing?" represent pseudo-problems. They are meaningless scientifically because they are logically impossible to answer. Incidentally, there has been no lack of such pseudo-problems in psychoanalysis which have wasted a huge amount of our scientific time (see page 73).

Assumptions. We realize today that, of necessity, science

makes certain assumptions which border on the metaphysical. We assume that the universe is ordered, that the order is discoverable and intelligible, that induction is safe, that there is a finite causality to events. These have been useful assumptions, but they are beliefs supported in turn by other beliefs whose underpinnings extend deep into nonrational convictions. Scientists say they believe only on the basis of facts, but then they accept only those facts which are congruent with certain beliefs. Occam's simplicity principle that assumed entities should not be multiplied beyond necessity stems from the wishful belief that nature is simple. And underlying all scientific activity is the human belief that it is good to know, to predict, and to control nature.

Structure of Scientific Theory. Finally there is a current view of a scientific theory as consisting of a hypothetico-deductive system in which high-level theoretical statements are linked through rules of interpretation to low-level observational statements.[10]

$$
\left. \begin{array}{c} \textit{Theoretical Statements} \\ \downarrow \qquad \uparrow \\ \textit{Observational Statements} \end{array} \right\} \text{Rules of Interpretation}
$$

The ideal system is such that observational statements are logically deducible from the theoretical statements. If the premises or assumptions in theoretical statements are of value, one can deduce and predict certain facts from them. If these predicted facts are then found through observation, the hypothetico-deductive system is considered to be of admirable usefulness in the description, explanation, prediction, and control of natural phenomena.

Since observational statements are of such underlying importance in the operation of this system, we will now attend to them in greater detail.

NOTES

1. For example, B. F. Skinner, "Critique of Psychoanalytic Concepts and Theories," in Herbert Feigl and Michael Scriven, Eds., *The Foundations of Science and the Concepts of Psychology and Psychoanalysis* (Minneapolis: University of Minnesota Press, 1956), Vol. I. Skinner's strictures and canons about psychoanalysis as a science are caustic, but the rest of this volume stands as a rejection of his position by philosophers of science.

2. Eysenck's shrill carping is quietly dissected in J. H. Woodger's *Physics, Psychology and Medicine* (Cambridge: Cambridge University Press, 1956).

3. One regularity found in the life histories of eminent scientists involves a school teacher under whose warm attentions the youngster's intellect blossoms. (See A. Roe, "A Psychologist Examines 64 Eminent Scientists," *Scientific American,* 187 [1952], 21-25.)

4. Fascinating clinical vignettes of scientists are described by L. S. Kubie in "Some Unsolved Problems of the Scientific Career," Parts I and II, *American Scientist,* 41 (1953), 596-613; 42 (1954), 104-112.

5. Although the prescriptions for success in science are often contradictory, the anecdotes about scientists are a delight. (See W. I. B. Beveridge, *The Art of Scientific Investigation* [New York: W. W. Norton & Co., Inc., 1957].)

6. The historical contrast between rationalism and empiricism is taken from H. Reichenbach, *The Rise of Scientific Philosophy* (Berkeley: University of California Press, 1951).

7. Three superb accounts of the scientific revolution can be found in the following books: A. Armitage, *The World of Copernicus* (New York: Mentor Books, 1956); H. Butterfield,

The Origins of Modern Science (London: G. Bell & Sons, Ltd., 1950); P. P. Wiener and A. Noland [Eds.], *Roots of Scientific Thought* (New York: Basic Books, 1957).

8. See T. Dantzig, *Number, The Language of Science* (New York: Doubleday Anchor Books, 1956). Einstein considered this the most interesting book on the evolution of mathematics he had ever read. It is a critical survey written for the "cultured nonmathematician."

9. Goedel's ingenuity in the original is unreadable to nonmathematicians. Hence, E. Nagel and J. R. Newman, "Goedel's Proof," in J. R. Newman (Ed.), *The World of Mathematics* (New York: Simon and Schuster, Inc., 1956), Vol. III, pp. 1668-1695.

10. This starkly deductive view of a scientific theory is described by R. B. Braithwaite, *Scientific Explanation* (Cambridge: Cambridge University Press, 1955).

:II:

Observation and Experiment

SCIENTIFIC OBSERVATION

To re-state it, a scientific theory offers a hypothetico-deductive system composed of high-level theoretical statements linked through interpretive rules of deductive inference to low-level observational statements.

In psychoanalysis our statements about drives, cathexis, or psychic apparatus would represent high-level theoretical statements about inferred, nonobservable entities. Our low-level observational statements refer to what persons actually say or do in the psychoanalytic situation. Thus our technical language, like other technical languages in science, is made up of a theory language and an observation language. To speak of a psychic apparatus, an "It," is to use theory language, whereas to speak of a person, a "He," is to use observation language.

Observation and Experiment

We have defined a scientist as a person who makes observations and/or experiments in order to collect data relevant to a hypothesis. If we consider experiments to be special ways of making systematic observations, we can condense the two temporarily under the general term "observation." We will now consider the nature of observation and observational statements for two important reasons: first, observations provide the empirical basis for psychoanalytic theories; second, our methods of observation in psychoanalysis call for improvement.

Scientific observation in general is characterized by three properties:

1. It is *systematic*. Of course, haphazard and chance observations occur in science and important discoveries have come about that way (for example, radium, penicillin), but they are rare. Scattered observations can be made in the course of more systematic observations guided by a specific hypothesis but it is the latter which have been the most fruitful.

2. It is *recorded*. Systematic observations must be recorded and not left victim to the fallibility of human memory. Scientists insist on recorded data because they are familiar with the unreliability of vaguely remembered impressions.

3. It is *controlled*. Various checks are applied to observations with respect to precision, objectivity, reliability (that is, can other observers make the same observations?), and validity (that is, do the observations concern what they are supposed to concern?).

Since scientific observation is relevant to some hypothesis, it begins with a systematic selection of some entity or feature out of all possible entities or features observable. In the psychoanalytic situation of patient and analyst there are a large number of interactional processes going on, some simultaneously, some continuously, and some discontinuously. Which ones should we select to observe, which ones are relevant to the investigative hypothesis, which ones can we ignore?

Let us use the standard clinical analytic situation to illustrate problems of systematizing, recording, and controlling observations.

SYSTEMATIZING

What should we observe in the clinical situation? The superclinician would reply "everything," but the myth of a perfect analyst is entitled to a rest. It is impossible to observe everything and for scientific purposes it is not even desirable. If we could observe everything we would pile up so much data that we could never manage it conceptually. We must *select* features or properties or variables *relevant* to a hypothesis concerning the problem under study. Once we have selected some qualitative feature for observation we must decide on its stable, invariant units. Suppose our research hypothesis asserts something about anxiety; we then want to make observations concerning anxiety in patients during the clinical analytic situation. Since anxiety is an affect-feeling directly observable only to the person experiencing it, an analyst must use behavioral criteria from which he can infer the presence of anxiety in a patient. The units of observation could then consist of motor, verbal, affective, and autonomic behaviors which indicate the presence of anxiety.

Under what conditions can these units of observation be identified? Anxiety may not be continuously present in patients in the clinical situation, but by listening to and looking at a patient we can follow his motor, verbal, affective, and autonomic behaviors and identify at what points in time and context behavioral indices of anxiety appear.

How can these units be measured and given some quantitative estimate? The first task in systematic observation would be a qualitative one of deciding what sorts of behavior will indicate the category of anxiety. The second task is a quantitative one of assigning some number or symbol to the category. For example, could we say that one discrete category of anxiety in a patient rates as 4 plus whereas in another patient it rates as only 1 plus? Or we might estimate anxiety in a given patient as a continuous category with different states having a quantifiable relation to one another; for example, state $A >$ state $B >$ state C.

Are the units of observation valid? Since the analytic observer of behavior is making an inference about a subjective experience of another person, the risk is that he may not be observing anxiety at all. The higher the level of inference, the greater is the risk of making invalid observations. Ideally, if both a theory and its measures are valid one can make successful testing predictions. In practice we can check our inference against the patient's self-observation by communicating it to him.

Are the units of observation reliable? If the units are stable, they can be repeatedly observed by us, and other observers witnessing the same behavioral phenomena can classify them as indications of, for example, anxiety.

RECORDING

The second property characteristic of scientific observation is that it is *recorded*. Freud did us a disservice as far as scientific efforts in psychoanalysis are concerned when he stated, "A reader who is willing to believe an analyst at all will give him credit for the touch of revision to which he has subjected his material." [1] If one is describing a case history at the clinical level of discourse, a touch of revision is acceptable enough. But at a scientific level of discourse, where we are concerned with a serious responsibility of confirming or establishing correct generalizations, this touch of revision must be rejected. Analysts should know better than anyone else the sorts of falsifications, distortions, and omissions which find a compressed refuge under the smallest "touches."

In the case of the Rat Man [2] Freud made notes on the evening of the day of treatment, an account which "adheres as closely as possible to my recollection of the patient's words." He warned that note-taking during the time of treatment harms the patient, through withdrawal of the physician's attention, more than the accuracy gained in recording the case history. Here we have in sharp focus the conflict between demands of pure and applied science. Pure science strives to establish correct generalization through testing hypotheses. If one depended on an hours-later memory of a complex series of events, only those events which favor a hypothesis might be remembered as the important ones. Observations should be recorded as soon as possible after the time of their occurrence. Freud regretted lacking a way "to make up for the deficiency of evidence found in psychoanalytic descriptions of cases." But nowadays we have a way—namely, tape recordings. For pure science the most reliable evidence of what takes place in the psychoanalytic situation is to be found on tape recordings supplemented by the analyst's notes regarding himself and the patient's nonverbal behavior.

When notebooks are kept of descriptions of observations we must select for phenomena word-names that have the same meanings for all the workers in a field. In the clinical situation, when a patient sweats, his hands and voice tremble, his facies are those of fear, and he describes his heart pounding, adding the information "I feel afraid of something now," we would all agree that these behaviors can be named "anxiety." It is when we get beyond directly observable categories into categories requiring a high degree of inference that the problem of naming becomes more difficult. For example, two analysts might differ on whether or not to label a patient's statement *not* mentioning the analyst as an indication of a transference reaction. Some statements directly indicate transference in their stated meaning-content whereas others, asserting nothing directly about the analyst, must be inferred to contain transference meaning.

CONTROLLING

The next problem is that of bias in scientific observation. We said initially that observation begins with a selection based on a tentative hypothesis. Darwin remarked, "How odd it is that anyone should not see that all observation must be for or against some view if it is to be of any service." The research hypothesis determining our selection operates to *exclude* as well as include observable features or properties. Such exclusions may constitute a serious distorting bias. Observations may be collected in a way that unhappily favors only one alternative hypothesis.

The trick is to arrange conditions of observation so that the selecting hypothesis first, does not have a serious distorting effect and second, allows room for alternative hypotheses to apply to the observations. For example, consider the early days of psychosomatic research when some of us were trying to correlate oral dependency with peptic ulcer. In every case of peptic ulcer we looked for oral dependency, neglecting other observations as trivial and limiting ourselves to the overly simple transitive equation, oral craving = food craving = gastric hyperactivity. Today we know the problem is more complex, that oral dependency is not a single entity, and that there are no one-to-one correlations between specific psychic wish and specific organ activity.

Fortunately we have ways of outwitting the inevitable bias of observation. We can apply a variety of checks and controls.[3] In investigating oral dependency-peptic ulcer relations, we must establish criteria for oral dependency, examine cases of other diseases for oral dependency, note cases of peptic ulcer without oral dependency, and study cases of oral dependency without peptic ulcer. We must scrutinize our activity to make sure that we are counting negative as well as positive instances of our hypothesis.

Besides self-scrutiny, another check consists of having multiple independent observers. Here we have a great but still untapped opportunity in psychoanalysis. Usually in other branches of psychology there are only a few investigators at one time observing for a few minutes or hours persons under similar conditions. But in psychoanalysis we have hundreds of analyst observers placing persons under highly similar and controlled conditions (the clinical analytic situation) and evaluating similar categories of behavior for months and years. The clinical analytic situation is so standardized in its essential aspects that we have a ready-made opportunity for multiple independent observers to compare recorded observations and to sort out the biasing effects of favored hypotheses.

Of course the assumption underlying a use of independent observers is that they are capable of truly independent judgments about reality. Observers might agree only because they share the same conceptual biases (or are friends) and not because what exists in external reality is the same. Again, in order to make reliable comparisons of what persons actually say and do in the psychoanalytic situation, we should compare tape recordings which allow us to start from agreed-on observation statements.

Kubie reports a neat example of a distortion discoverable only by the use of tapes.[4] In presenting tape-recorded sessions the therapist reported that at a certain point the patient asked to have the tape recorder turned off. However, on listening to the recording of the session, it was actually the therapist who suggested the machine be turned off, not the patient.

Besides flaws of distortion and false addition in records written after a session, there occur flaws of omission. Often too many events occur with such split-second rapidity that an analyst cannot note them all down, especially when he is under pressure to make some response in the form of a therapeutic intervention. Also, at these moments he is too close to the events to judge their relative long-run significance, so that his selection may result in serious omissions.

Finally, an important pure-science advantage to tape recordings is that we can study events of the analytic situation at our leisure, when we are under no pressure to respond to them. We can restudy tapes over and over to uncover new aspects. Other analyst observers can listen to them and recheck the findings. There still exists a resistance among some analysts against the use of tape recordings. I do not think it is for fear of violating the *patient's* privacy that analysts object. This sort of resistance is motivated by analysts' fears of exposure. They become used to working in solitary grandeur with a majestic authority unchallenged except by forces easily dismissed with the label "neurotic." It is not easy for analysts to subject their hard-earned but quickly gained surety to public scrutiny. Strange, that one whose career consists of peering into other persons' most private data does not want to be peered at while doing so. But we will overcome this resistance in ourselves as we witness colleagues suffering the same embarrassments as our own and as we become wise to those self-righteous scolds who perpetuate the paragon myth.

AGAIN, THE BOGY

Scientific observation, besides being systematic, recorded, and controlled, should also be quantitative. Numbers and other symbols are used in descriptions of observations. They allow a more precise description and ultimately may make possible mathematical operations for manipulating symbols according to rules.

Numbers such as the simple 1 and 0 can be used to indicate the presence or absence of anxiety during some time stretch in psychoanalytic treatment, and number can be used to represent the total. Or we might use numbers to represent degrees of anxiety: mild = 1, moderate = 2, and severe = 3. Notice that these are rank orders. Category 3, severe anxiety, does not indicate three times as much anxiety as category 1. We do not need elaborate statistical methods in psychoanalysis. Computing simple means and percentages often suffices when we deal with populations rather than random samples.

Certainly one can overdo a mathematical approach. Wiener, a mathematician, said, "No self-respecting scientist has any right to give the impression of a mathematical analysis of difficult situations, unless he is using language which he can understand and which he can apply correctly. Short of this, a purely descriptive account of the gross appearance of a phenomenon is both more honest and more scientific." [5]

It is not that all descriptions in science must ideally be numerical. If a word is sufficient for the purpose of an investigation, it is ridiculous to use a number. If it suffices to call the blood red, it is fatuous to describe it by a table of wave lengths. In the clinical situation, it is usually sufficient to describe a patient as anxious rather than give numerical values of skin temperature and pulse rate and number of voice tremors per second. The threat of pseudo-rigor and number magic is not yet a serious one in psychoanalysis, however. Our troubles still lie in the correct use of a technical English language rather than a technical mathematical language.

To be complete I should mention that scientific observation often uses, as aids, such instruments as microscopes, telescopes, stethoscopes. As yet we have no observational instruments in psychoanalysis other than tape recorders and cameras. We use the unaided ear and eye to pick up sound and light waves. Our problem lies not in receiving accurately signals of sufficient intensity but in decoding these signals into messages of meaning. We have no need to magnify our observables further. Our need is to decode human messages accurately and to select the ones most meaningfully relevant to the problem at hand. It is possible to invent a mechanical decoder of messages, but so far the human brain is the most compact, efficient, and powerful decoder of human messages yet discovered.

EXPERIMENTAL OBSERVATION

Thus far we have been discussing what can be called "naturalistic" observation, that is, observation of natural processes uninterfered with by an observer except for the disturbance produced by all observation. There is another type of observation called "experimental," in which the observer actively and systematically interferes with natural processes in order to increase his knowledge about them.

Experimental observation remains an underdeveloped aspect of psychoanalysis. Admittedly it is difficult to experiment with persons. First, how to interfere with natural processes in persons without doing violence to the phenomena being investigated represents a complicated problem. Second, persons have minds of their own which can make a shambles of "controlled" experimental conditions. And third, to tamper with the mental life of persons raises ethical questions which, if they become loud enough, can jeopardize the personal safety of an investigator in his community. In spite of these difficulties, the psychoanalytic investigator should strive resolutely but sensibly to utilize every appropriate scientific method which has a chance of increasing his knowledge.

Experiments are special ways of making observations with some degree of control over the variables involved and over conditions under which they are studied. In an experiment, specific observations are actualized or induced by the investigator. Hence an experiment is a type of active observation in contrast to passive naturalistic observation in which one must wait for certain events to occur naturally. Because they involve vigorous, meddlesome action, experiments can bring to light phenomena usually beyond the range of naturalistic observation.

The clinical analytic situation in some respects approaches an experimental situation. Psychoanalytic treatment can be viewed as a series of small daily experiments under relatively controlled conditions. I will discuss this in greater detail in Chapter IV.

There are two sorts of experiments in science: The first are nature's experiments, when real-life circumstances interfere with what we believe to be a natural course of events—for example, when a laborer has a crowbar accidentally driven through his forebrain or when, during the London bombings, children were separated from their mothers and sent to nurseries in the country. These are termed "nature's experiments" since the interference is not produced intentionally by an investigator but results from the accidents of real life. The second are pure or contrived experiments, when exact conditions are created by an investigator and then interfered with systematically. Some variables are kept constant while others are manipulated by being inserted or withdrawn or both. Such experiments are designed by the investigator to answer a specific question through deliberate interferences in an artificial, simplified situation. The experimental situation, being contrived and artificially simplified, is quite different from real-life and naturally occurring situations.

The interference introduced in an experiment is called the independent, or experimental, or input variable. We observe and measure the effect of the input variable on a dependent, or response, or output variable. An experiment represents an attempt at a systematic and controlled study of interrelationships between input and output variables. We search for concomitant variation between input and output or we compare a process before and after input or we compare two groups of which one receives an input and the other does not.

It is usually stated that a planned experiment has the advantages that the investigator is fully prepared to make observations because he actualizes the conditions under which they appear, that the experiment can be repeated by the investigator and by others because the conditions are known and creatable, and that the investigator can vary input variables systematically because they are under his control and can note variations in the output variables.

All this represents a somewhat idealized description of the planned experiment. The ideal classical experiment of two-variable design is seldom achieved even in the hard sciences such as physics or chemistry. In the softer sciences of medicine and psychology it is probably impossible to attain the ideal degree of control and precision. But through modern experimental design and statistics we can handle problems of multiple variables and of ever-present uncertainties. Also exciting are new prospects of programing computers to simulate human thought processes and other psychic state-sequences. For this would provide us a more ideal experimental opportunity to manipulate antecedent variables such as stored memories.

In psychological experiments it may be difficult to create a contrived or laboratory situation strong enough to get measurable results. The experiment may be correctly designed but yield negative results because reactions in the experimental subjects are not strong enough. We know that in the clinical analytic situation we observe and evoke strong affective reactions like those that occur in real-life situations. We must remember that *for the patient* the psychoanalytic situation is a real-life situation of great import. Patients who come to analysis are strongly motivated to seek help for crucial problems which are highly consequential for their whole life course. Under such conditions we are bound to observe events which do not appear in questionnaire responses or in eye-wink experiments.

Previously I mentioned that psychoanalysts have a ready-made opportunity to compare observations of multiple observers because of the standardized nature of the analytic situation. This situation also provides psychoanalysts with an experimental opportunity, since it represents a planned, artificially simplified situation in which, just as in real life, strong reactions are evoked. A relationship develops between analyst and patient in which the patient experiences strong positive and negative feelings. They share in regular, intimate, private, and often intense human interactions with crucial fluctuations over prolonged periods of time. The analyst de-

signs and carries out deliberate interferences with this interaction through controlled and selected spoken inputs. Finally,
notice one other similarity to the laboratory experiment. The
events studied in this two-person interaction take place in
the convenient privacy of one small room. Our observables
in psychoanalysis are of such manageable dimensions that
we do not have to go outside of one room as does a field
worker in anthropology or social psychology.

A description of the role of experiments has been summarized in the language of information theory as follows.[6]
In naturalistic observation we receive messages from nature
in an unknown code and we try to break the code. An experiment puts a question to nature, who responds in the
code. Questions represent probes designed to evoke simple
and decisive answers. Since we can choose the questions we
can design them to get simple answers in code. The best
way to break a code and understand it is to start with simple
units and gradually build from them the larger units.

I have tried to emphasize the advantages of experimental
observation in scientific inquiry. This does not entail a
neglect of naturalistic clinical observation, which is still our
primary source of data. Medicine would not have advanced
very far if it relied only on experimental knowledge. It is
through a combination of clinical and experimental approaches that we will advance our knowledge of human behavior.

An Introduction to Psychoanalytic Research

A FABLE

How do we use naturalistic and experimental observation in science? In Chapter I, I said we used observations to test the tenability of hypotheses. Let us take a fictive hypothesis to illustrate this testing.

Suppose our hypothesis asserts that two variables, *A* and *B*, have some systematic interrelation under certain specified conditions. Let us say a Trobriander (Malinowski angered psychoanalysts to the point that now Trobrianders leap to our minds whenever we think of primitives) asserts that beating tom-toms at dusk makes the sun disappear and brings on nightfall. The naturalistic observational evidence for this hypothesis is overwhelming because every evening for a thousand years the tribe has beaten tom-toms at dusk and the sun has gone down. We must agree with our primitive scientist that the supporting evidence for his hypothesis is impressive.

But we say to him, "This evidence, though of enormous size, is not sufficient to be confirmatory. Let us test your hypothesis by an experiment. The advantage of an experiment in this case is that we can manipulate variable *A*, tom-tom beating. We create *A*, say at noon, and fail to produce *B*, nightfall."

"Wait!" cries the Trobriander. "The hypothesis asserts that under certain conditions, namely dusk, *A* produces *B*. You don't have the right conditions when you create *A* at noon."

"Well-scored," we reply. "If *A* at dusk, then *B*. But we have another way of manipulating *A*. Let us prevent *A* at dusk and see if this prevents *B*." So we do not beat tom-toms at dusk, and we note that nightfall comes on anyway. Through this experiment we have tested the hypothesis and found it to be untenable. Incidentally, this example illustrates the difference between a sufficient cause (create *A* and get *B*) and a necessary cause (prevent *A* and get no *B*).

If a hypothesis asserts two events or states are regularly conjoined and they can be shown through naturalistic and experimental observation to vary in predicted ways, then the hypothesis is tenable and constitutes a good explanation of the conjunction between the two events or states.

EXPLANATION

What is an explanation in science? It is as difficult to explain explanation as it is to explain anything else. But using the *If A, then B* model let us have at the traditional answer.

A good scientific explanation satisfies the criteria (1) *If you produce A, then you will get B.* (2) *If you prevent A, then you will get no B.* This represents an ideal explanation by a lawlike principle. If you can confirm both *A* and *B*, it is considered a strong explanation. But if one cannot confirm *A*, the explanation is open to the fallacy of affirming the consequent, namely, *If A, then B; B is true, therefore A.* The fallacy lies in the fact that many events other than *A* could have given rise to *B*. Hence it is argued that often in natural science one cannot verify true hypotheses, one can only refute false ones as follows: *If A, then B; but not B, therefore not A.* Only when we can confirm both *A* and *B* do we avoid this common logical error.

When working with an individual patient an analyst constructs explanations by methods of colligation and internal consistency of evidence. He connects events into a pattern and intrinsically relates the pattern to other patterns. From these explanation sketches regarding individuals, generalizations regarding a class are attempted and lawlike explanations are formulated.

When we have a generalization such that we can combine it with a specific case to predict a future state of the case, then we have a good explanation. Water boils when heated. Here is a can of water. If we heat it, the water will boil. We can predict a future state of a member of a class by combining it with a generalization that holds for the entire class.

The danger lies in generalizations which provide pseudo-explanations. A pseudo-explanation simply describes the same phenomenon with two different sets of verbal terms. Suppose we ask for an explanation of why a man is unmarried and are told, "Because he is a bachelor." Following our model, A stands for being a bachelor and B stands for being unmarried. If you produce A, then you will get B. But how is A different from B? The state "bachelor" does not explain the state "unmarried." They are both descriptions of the single state.

Since all of our definitions in psychoanalysis are still verbal (and not yet mathematical), we must be on guard against pseudo-explanations. You can read in our literature "explanations" such as this: "If there is a weak ego, there will be depersonalization." As evidence for the presence of a weak ego the author will then point to depersonalization. This constitutes an unsatisfactory explanation because "depersonalization" is used only as another way of describing a weak ego. If criteria for a weak ego could be stated and the prediction made that whenever you find this state you will also find depersonalization, then the explanation would be a more satisfactory one.

The idea of prediction is often involved in describing what constitutes scientific explanation. There is a current controversy over the role of prediction in explanation.[7] It may not be necessary that an explanatory generalization, in order to be good, must allow predictions to be made regarding specific cases and make it possible to bring such cases under the generalization. We can explain earthquakes and evolution but we cannot predict a specific earthquake or a direction in which a species will evolve.

In its general sense, prediction means to announce some event prior to knowledge of its occurrence. A prediction may involve an event occurring before or after the time of making the predicting statement. In listening to a patient narrate some events of his childhood, you may predict, in your own mind, that in adolescence he turned to another family for parental support. Or in case supervision one may notice that a supervising analyst will make surprising predictions as to the course an analysis took weeks ago. We call these retrodictions, but they are forms of predictions since they occur prior to knowledge of an event.

THE BRAVE SEMMELWEISS

To illustrate an interplay of observation, intuition, experiment, reasoning, explanation, and prediction in scientific inquiry, let us pause to consider the story of Semmelweiss.[8] It is not a happy one and that is perhaps why we still can feel the thrust and impact of his triumphs and disasters.

The problem was childbed fever and the portion of the world of experience was the medical care of women after they had delivered their babies in hospitals. A few days after delivery, women with childbed, or puerperal, fever suffered chills, high fever, and delirium leading in many cases to death. The disease increased in the seventeenth, eighteenth, and nineteenth centuries as more and more women, at the insistence of their doctors, came into hospitals for delivery. It was a disease occurring in hospitals but rarely in home deliveries. It was a disease of civilized people and not of primitives. From one in five to one in twenty mothers died of it. For a year not a mother in the Italian province of Lombardy survived it. What was the explanation?

In the nineteenth century there were several hypotheses proposed to explain the disease. It was attributed to lochial suppression. A scanty lochial discharge caused puerperal fever. (Today we know the converse is true. It is puerperal fever which leads to a scanty discharge). Milk retention was also blamed and there were even descriptions in medical textbooks of milk pneumonia, milk meningitis, and milk peritonitis. Anxiety over childbirth was another suggestion.

Hypotheses about atmospheric-telluric epidemics were perhaps the favorites of the time.

In 1795 a Scots physician, Alexander Gordon, proposed that the fever was due to a specific contagion. He noted the disease occurred only in those attended by a physician or a nurse who had previously attended patients with the disease. He even called it erysipelas, and today we know how closely the two are related. In 1829 Collins, an Englishman, showed that by antisepsis the mortality could be reduced to 0.53 per cent in 10,000 cases, but no one paid any attention to him either. Our own Oliver Wendell Holmes believed in the contagionist hypothesis, but it met little acceptance from other medical men. Why? Apart from the usual human inertia, there was the factor that the contagionist hypothesis incriminated doctors. It implied that they somehow caused or spread the disease. Denial is a front-line defense against guilt.

Semmelweiss was a Hungarian obstetrician (he was not Jewish, as many who know of his sufferings automatically assume) working in the Vienna General Hospital. In 1846 he was in charge of the first of two charity clinics. The First Clinic, staffed by physicians and medical students, had a mortality rate four times that of the Second Clinic, which was staffed by midwives and student midwives. Patients were randomly assigned to the clinics according to available bed space. Since the presence of childbed fever and of death is easily established, Semmelweiss had a simple quantitative measure to rely on.

Semmelweiss clung to one strong observation in testing

hypotheses about childbed fever: the fact that the two clinics had a markedly different mortality rate. If the disease was due to some atmospheric influence, why did it operate in the First Clinic and not in the Second? They were in the same building and subject to the same atmospheric conditions. Also, these atmospheric conditions held for homes as well as hospitals, but when a rise in the disease occurred in hospitals there was no rise in nearby homes. Semmelweiss seemingly demonstrated the atmospheric hypothesis to be untenable in the face of the evidence. Yet, twenty-five years after he gave the correct explanation, physicians still held the atmospheric hypothesis. Even the great Virchow believed it as late as 1858, although in 1865, sixteen years after Semmelweiss's demonstration, he finally accepted the contagion hypothesis as a correct explanation.

When it was proposed that the disease resulted from overcrowding in hospitals, Semmelweiss again used his one strong fact to refute the hypothesis. There were more women in the Second Clinic than in the First. The high mortality of the First Clinic was so well known in Vienna that women begged (picture these heart-rending scenes) not to be assigned there. Hence the beds of the Second Clinic were always filled.

Some believed the mothers were so frightened at being in the First Clinic that they developed childbed fever. Deaths were frequent there and the priest came tolling his little bell often. But Semmelweiss knew that the reputation of the First Clinic came from the high mortality rate which then secondarily aroused anxiety. Also, he asked the priest to dispense with his bell (as a possible anxiety arousing factor); its elimination, however, had no effect on the disease rate.

Semmelweiss examined hypotheses regarding ventilation of the two clinics, their linen, their temperature, and the procedures of their staffs. The midwives used the lateral position for delivery; physicians used the dorsal position. Semmelweiss, through a great effort plus a night and day watch, induced physicians to use the lateral position for a time, but the experiment failed, mortality and morbidity remaining the same. Forceps were used in both clinics, but most of the births did not involve forceps. Primiparas developed the disease more often than multiparas. But there was a low incidence of the disease among primiparas who delivered in the street on the way to the hospital, despite much dirtier conditions.

As Semmelweiss thus worked, testing hypotheses through naturalistic and experimental observation, he came to favor contagion theories. At this point he was demoted by his superior Klein, who had in his textbook demolished the contagion theory to his satisfaction. Klein didn't like Semmelweiss's ideas or his personality. (Science involves personalities as much as any other human activity. The myths of truth being our only judge, of ability being justly rewarded, of noble men dispassionately viewing one another's work are promoted by people like Klein.)

Semmelweiss went on a vacation. While he was away a friend and senior colleague died of pyemia following a wound received during pathology dissection. Semmelweiss returned to the autopsy of his friend and was struck by the similarity of these autopsy findings with those of childbed fever patients. It occurred to him that perhaps some sort of cadaveric particles (which could not be seen) were transferred to mothers by doctors who did autopsies. Klein, as head of the department, insisted that his staff spend time each morning dissecting in the pathology laboratory. Klein's predecessor had not been so insistent, and during his reign the mortality rate in the clinics was quite low.

Although the cadaveric particles were not visible, Semmelweiss guessed that they must be present even after hand-washing because one could smell the cadaver on hands for hours. The cadaveric particle hypothesis began to fit the evidence. In the First Clinic, physicians and students who did dissections brought in the infection. The midwives of the Second Clinic performed no dissections and hence were not contaminated. Also, the few physicians attending the Second Clinic did not go to the pathology laboratory.

Now Semmelweiss made a type of prediction (retrodiction) that when there was a physician in the Second Clinic who did dissections, the mortality rate must have risen. He checked back in the records and found a period when the head of the Second Clinic was a man who dissected frequently. During this period, the mortality rate in the Second Clinic was at its highest.

Other observations fell in line under Semmelweiss's explanation. It had been observed that the mothers sickened in rows of beds rather than across aisles. Why? Because they were examined in rows by physicians and students on rounds. Also, there was little puerperal fever in street births because the mothers, once delivered, were not examined by doctors.

In attempting to refute Semmelweiss's hypothesis, Virchow claimed that weather was an important factor, since the incidence of puerperal fever was highest in winter. But Semmelweiss showed that it was in winter that physicians and students spent the most time dissecting cadavers.

Semmelweiss made another retrodiction regarding himself. While he was away the mortality had been as low as 1.9 per cent in February. When he got his job back (friends helped), the mortality began to rise again and by April it rose to 18.2 per cent. Why? Semmelweiss himself was an ardent dissector who diligently worked in the pathology lab every morning. He was more responsible than anyone for transferring cadaveric particles!

All this was supporting evidence which tended to confirm Semmelweiss's hypothesis. But, as with the Trobriander's tom-toms, an experimental manipulation of variables is called for before the hypothesis can be considered a satisfactory explanation of the if A, then B kind. If we prevent A (the cadaveric particles), keeping all other conditions the same, then we should not get B (childbed fever). Semmelweiss instituted a policy in which all physicians and students had to wash their hands in a chlorine solution which, again using the sense of smell as a measure, removed the cadaver odor and hypothetical particles.

I will not elaborate on Semmelweiss's heroic struggles to see to it that doctors did as he ordered. (It can be left to imagination.) By July the mortality dropped to 1.2 per cent. The experimental test was repeated in other hospitals and confirmed the hypothesis. In Budapest the mortality was reduced to 0.85 per cent. Nor will I go into the tragic effects Semmelweiss's discovery had on his life. Semmelweiss became depressed and eventually paranoid. He was taken to a mental hospital where he died in a few days of streptococcal septicemia initiated by a wound he received at pathology dissection. He died like the friend whose autopsy gave him his hunch and like the mothers of the First Clinic whom he struggled to save. To read of the personal envies, rivalries, vanity, and sabotage that embroiled Semmelweiss's efforts is truly saddening to anyone with high ideals for human nature. The reception of a correct explanation is a matter quite different from its discovery and confirmation. We learn over and over from history that we do not learn from history. To compel assent from scientists, an explanation must have more than correctness. It must have appeal.

NOTES

1. One measure of a great man consists of how long his errors are perpetuated. The scientific disservice is from S. Freud, "Recommendations for Physicians on the Psychoanalytic Method of Treatment," *Collected Papers* (New York: Basic Books, 1959), Vol. II, pp. 323-333.

2. S. Freud, "Notes upon a Case of Obsessional Neurosis," *Collected Papers* (New York: Basic Books, 1959), Vol. III, pp. 293-383.

3. A succinct and superlative account of the problem of controls is offered in Group for the Advancement of Psychiatry, "Some Observations on Controls in Psychiatric Research," *Report No. 42*, 1959.

4. This fantastic but credible error is described in L. S. Kubie, "Research into the Process of Supervision in Psychoanalysis," *Psychoanalytic Quarterly*, 27 (1958), 226-236.

5. It is mathematicians who must constantly remind us of the limitations of their discipline. (See N. Wiener, "Some Maxims for Biologists and Psychologists," *Dialectia*, 4 [1950], 22-27.)

6. Several chapters in this volume sparkle with succinct presentations of complex areas. (J. Bronowski, "Science as Foresight," in J. R. Newman [Ed.], *What Is Science?* [New York: Simon and Schuster, 1955].)

7. The prediction-explanation controversy rolls on in the *British Journal of Philosophy of Science*. For example, see N. Rescher, "On Prediction and Explanation," *British Journal of The Philosophy of Science*, 8 (1958), 281-290.

8. The account of Semmelweiss's struggle to solve a tangled problem is from F. G. Slaughter, *Immortal Magyar* (New York: Henry Schuman, 1950).

:III:

Psychoanalysis as Science

A CRITIQUE

HAVING SKIMMED through some elementary scientific principles, we now come to that particular portion of the world of experience interesting to scientific psychoanalysts. There is no need to ancestor-worship Freud any more than is being done. But as the first psychoanalyst his views on psychoanalysis as science should be of interest to us.

"As a specialized science, a branch of psychology—'depth psychology' or psychology of the unconscious—it [psychoanalysis] is quite unsuited to form a Weltanschauung of its own; it must accept that of science in general. . . .

"The contribution of psycho-analysis to science consists precisely in having extended research to the region of the mind." [1]

Psychoanalysis as Science

Psychoanalysis began as an effort which qualified as early science with pure and applied aspects. Since it also began in medicine, a practical art, it was soon taken over by medical organization men unappreciative of pure science needs. Although psychoanalysis today is mainly a medical guild, it realizes that, in order to progress, it must nourish its pure science roots and work at the discovery of new knowledge. As the investigative spirit grows within psychoanalysis and it becomes estimable to search for concepts and observations which may even replace Freud's, we will begin to advance beyond him, as every field must in time supersede its great men.

We claim that psychoanalysis is a branch of science. But others assert that science and psychoanalysis are antithetical. Here I am not thinking of ignorant or slanderous or pathological critics but of informed scientists willing to give a hearing to psychoanalytic knowledge-claims. Darwin mentioned that he always noted down what informed critics had to say, otherwise he might easily forget it. So let us review what our critics point out, lest we forget.[2]

Uncontrolled Observation. They assert that our hypotheses guiding observation are favored by the way in which we make observations. We miss or neglect as trivial other observations which fail to support a hypothesis. Because, in the special nature of the analytic situation, the analyst is the sole observer, one has to accept his observations, hoping that he is self-critical and self-monitoring. But in the analytic situation strong emotions are evoked in the observer as well as the observed, and the analyst's own emotional needs may bias his observations. The emotional need that involves him in the psychoanalytic guild can induce theoretical biases that tend to perpetuate traditional concepts. For example, witness how analysts cling to dualistic instinct theory—or worse, to an Eros-Thanatos theory—in spite of all the evidence against them, both logical and empirical.

Unrecorded Observations. Analysts do not keep accurate records of observations. They rely too often on vaguely remembered impressions. When they keep written records, they are vainly trying to capture split-second events and complex moments which never reoccur exactly. In a field in which experimental observation is so limited, all the more attention should be paid to recording and standardizing naturalistic observations.

Lack of Quantification. To weigh the statistical significance and reliability of observations one needs quantitative estimates. But psychoanalysts neglect the measurement of quantities and seldom use statistics. In a field lacking experiments and having small numbers of cases, small-sample statistics should be used to obtain necessary precision.

Lack of Experiment. Analysts do not experiment in any controlled way. They rely on naturalistic observation and correlation only, which limits them to formulating unreliable causal generalizations. Psychoanalytic treatment is only a crude approach to an experiment which lacks design, control, and systematic variation of factors.

Lack of Control. Psychoanalysts do not compare their patient group with other groups. Hence the therapeutic changes observed might occur in a matched group. Lacking standards for comparison, we cannot be sure that psycho-analytic treatment is at all effective.

Lack of Follow-up. Psychoanalysts do not make systematic attempts to follow up their cases at five-, ten-, twenty-year intervals. They leave it to chance whether they will see or hear about a patient years later.

Lack of Confirmation. Psychoanalysts report a single case or four to five cases, state a hypothesis regarding some prob-lem the cases illustrate, and then end the matter there, as if the hypothesis is now worthy of acceptance. Such a hy-pothesis may be accepted not because of the evidence but rather because of the standing in his field of the analyst who proposes it. Sometimes a proposed hypothesis is mistaken for a fact and even used as evidence supporting a second hypothesis. Before a hypothesis can be accepted there must be further observations made on other cases by other analysts.

Lack of Predictive Value of Theories. Psychoanalysts state that certain childhood experiences produce certain neurotic states. One should be able to predict that, if certain experi-ences occur in a child he will become thus and so. Also, if we observe a certain neurotic state, we should be able to predict that the patient had this or that childhood experience. However neither of these predictions can be made with accuracy.

Lack of Interpretive Rules. There are no clear, intersub-jectively shared lines of reasoning between theories and ob-servations. The same observed phenomena will elicit many different interpretations from different analysts. Many of these interpretations are not compatible with one another.

If analysts themselves cannot agree that a given observation is an example of a certain theory, then the rules governing psychoanalytic inferences are unreliable.

Obscurantist Language. Although every specialized science must have its technical language, psychoanalysis indulges in allegorical and metaphorical statements which have no scientific meaning. In psychoanalytic writing, literary, metaphysical, and poetic terms abound with no clear relation between a term and its referent.

All these criticisms are justifiable to some degree, and worth our attention. More important, they are constructive criticisms of shortcomings about which we can do something. The remedy consists of better methods of recording observations, systematic study of more relevant variables in the psychoanalytic situation, better research designs, theory explication with closer ties between observables and constructs, and the use of experimental methods. We can better our efforts rather than resign ourselves to insuperable difficulties inherent to the subject matter. Of course, some people still maintain that psychoanalysis can never become a science because of the particular nature of its subject matter. Their argument runs: "Psychoanalysis deals with the private data of thoughts and feelings, whereas science is concerned with public data. Introspection is too unreliable a basis on which to build a science." This view fails to realize, however, that all science begins with private data which is made public by verbalizing it. A scientist examines what he can observe in his own consciousness and describes it in a language, whether the "it" is the color green or a memory of yesterday. Science becomes objective through intersubjective consistency—that is, many scientists describe finding similar entities in their conscious awareness. A psychoanalyst hears descriptions of contents of consciousness from persons observing themselves. If we find regularities in these descriptions, then we have the necessary basis for the formulation of explanatory principles.

We can make a science out of psychoanalytic data and theory if we work to eliminate the errors subject to correction. Psychoanalysis as a science will belong to the community of sciences and hence will have neighbors with whom investigators should be acquainted.

INTEGRATIVE LEVELS

Philosophers of science have used a concept of integrative levels to describe relations between scientific disciplines. This concept involves an ascending order of complexity, from a small entity such as an electron to a large entity such as the United Nations. One can draw up a table showing a range of entities and a methodological hierarchy (see page 58). There is much overlapping among neighboring scientific disciplines, since the divisions between entities are not sharp. Concepts, methods, and even observations are borrowed from both upstairs and downstairs neighbors.

If we consider that all of these entities play some part in effecting human behavior, we can conveniently subdivide them into separate domains of things, organisms, and per-

AN INTEGRATIVE SCALE

	Entity	Discipline
	Species	Anthropology, ethology, paleontology, population statistics
	Community	Sociology, ecology, anthropology, economics
Domain of Persons	Small group	Group psychology, linguistics, sociology
	Family	Social psychiatry, psychoanalysis, psychology
	Diad	Psychoanalysis, psychology, psychotherapy, communication theory
	Person	Psychoanalysis, psychology, psychiatry, medicine
Domain of Organisms	Organ	Neurophysiology, psychopharmacology, embryology
	Cell	Cytology, biophysics, pathology, genetics
	Organelle	Histology, histochemistry
Domain of Things	Molecule	Biochemistry, biophysics
	Atom	Physics, chemistry

sons. Psychoanalysis is concerned with the domain of persons, in particular the effect of person on person.

We can learn from both upstairs and downstairs neighbors on the integrative scale. No one has an imperialistic monopoly on knowledge useful for the understanding of human behavior. Many disciplines contribute to the science of persons. These contributions should be evaluated regardless of the status of the contributor. By title Pasteur was not a physician, Freud was not a psychologist, and Copernicus was not an astronomer (he was a physician). A plant physi-

efk · g5 – Comparative Animal ... or

ologist may solve the problem of cancer and a communication theorist the problem of psychotherapeutic change.

There are a few neighboring disciplines we should keep up close acquaintances with. They work on problems relevant to ours and they have interesting things to say about determinants of human behavior.

Neurophysiology. We all feel that the brain or central nervous system is the organ of mind. The brain is the material structure whose functioning gives rise to the event structure which generates patterns of observable behavior. The brain is to behavior what geography is to history—it provides the theater for events.

There are new movements taking place in neurophysiology. The old-time neurophysiologist was interested in the brain as just a brain, an organ to be studied for its peculiarities. But modern neurophysiologists are interested in the brain *as it regulates human behavior.* The discovery of reticular activating and diencephalic systems as diffuse sensory projection systems represents an example of the new views of neurophysiology. The work of Dement[3] on dreaming is of great relevance for psychoanalysis. We should pause to read any paper by Magoun, McLean, or Gerard.[4]

Correlations between mind as events and brain as matter are still difficult. Translation of the unknowns of one discipline into the unknowns of another does not get us very far. For a comprehensive, brilliant, and elegant discussion of the whole mind-brain problem, see Feigl.[5]

Ethology. Ethologists, who study comparative animal behavior, are close neighbors of psychoanalysts, since they too focus on patterns of events in time rather than patterns of matter in space. Since they are concerned directly with the behavior of individual organisms they are even closer neighbors than those neurophysiologists who are more organ-bound than behavior-bound.

The work of current animal ethology bears on instinctual drive constructs in psychoanalysis, on the drive (innate) *mneme* (experiential) relation and on the pluralistic classification of drives. It has not advanced us to say that all behavior is to some extent learned and to some extent innate in origin. We want to know more precisely what is autogenous (preferable to "innate"), when it operates (because a pattern appears months or years after birth does not necessarily mean it is learned), and how it dominates or submits to the learned experiential. In studying the autogenous maturation of differentiated species-specific patterns, ethologists have the advantage of experimental methods but the disadvantage of poor communication with their experimental subjects.

Too, ethologists are neighbors in a conceptual sense, for they went through some of the same stages of theoretical awkwardness as those encountered in psychoanalysis. For example, a few years ago some ethologists utilized a hydraulic energy construct which they have now abandoned—with, I think it fair to say, far greater ease than most psychoanalysts have been able to do. Current efforts in ethology attempt to conceptualize critical phases in development and the regulation of conflict, both of which are leading problems in psychoanalysis also. For further information read Bowlby, Fletcher, or Schiller. [6]

Psychology. First among our upstairs neighbors are psychologists. There is now a revival of interest in learning theory among them and they are turning to an evaluation of the psychoanalytic psychology of child development. Also they study conflict and its regulation under the terms of cognitive dissonance—for example, Festinger.[7] The effect of person on person, which has been the field mainly of psychotherapists and psychoanalysts, is receiving more systematic consideration—here, for example, see Heider.[8] It is psychologists who have developed and refined statistics for small samples and who can help us with problems of research design (Hall and Lindzey).[9]

Anthropology. This neighbor has perhaps been more effected by psychoanalysis than contributing to it—for example, see LaBarre.[10] However, like ourselves, anthropologists, deal with patterns of human behavior, particularly those patterns shared by many individuals of a group. These internalized normative patterns are the basis for certain regularities in the group and insure socially predictable behavior from its individuals.

Linguistics is an important branch of modern anthropology. The Whorf-Lee-Sapir-Von Humboldt-Abelard hypothesis regarding language as a determinant of one's view of reality has been of interest to psychoanalysts. The hypothesis is now looked on with some reserve, and evidence from the jargon aphasias tends to contradict it, but it stands as an example of a problem area shared by psychoanalysis and anthropology.

An Introduction to Psychoanalytic Research

The study of universals, of invariant patterns holding for all persons in all groups, is of special relevance for psychoanalytic constructs regarding ideal or healthy mental functioning. See Kluckhohn in *Anthropology Today* (edited by Kroeber) [11] and also Kluckhohn in Hall and Lindzey. By the way, the universal incest taboo still presents many unsolved problems for both fields.[12]

Neighbors also fight occasionally, and some anthropologists attack us as reductionist enemies who want to reduce culture (normative patterns) to psychology. Their fear is to some extent justified by Freud's statement that there are only two sciences: natural science and psychology (pure and applied). Sociology and anthropology would then be the study of psychologically motivated behavior of man in a society. Psychoanalysis and anthropology start with similar observations, human behavior patterns, including linguistic reports. Clinical psychoanalysis is concerned with those patterns in conflict in an individual person. These patterns may or may not be normative. Anthropology concerns itself with group-shared normative patterns. General psychoanalysis is now interested in all patterns of human behavior, thus embracing both sociology and anthropology, who may feel the embrace too presumptuous.

Communication Theory. One discipline relevant to psychoanalysis, communication theory, arose in the domain of things rather than in the domain of organisms or persons. Engineering problems in telegraphy and wire communication have produced a group of workers who are now our newest neighbors.

[62]

Psychoanalysis as Science

First, they are concerned with an entity with which we deal constantly, namely, information. Information is not matter and it is not energy. It is knowledge in some symbolic form which is exchanged through messages by communicating persons. Second, communication theorists have concepts, such as message, symbols, and code, which are suitable to conceptualize interactions between patient and analyst in the analytic situation. For example, when we speak of therapeutic change as involving structural change, we mean a change in the patient's time-enduring psychic functions; these can be thought of as making up a structural code. Psychoanalysts receive information from patients who, in describing their contents of conscious awareness, send messages which can be decoded. When an analyst intervenes, he sends messages to the patient which when decoded will gradually produce revisions in his beliefs and, ultimately, his behavior patterns.

But here the neighbors diverge. For psychoanalysts are concerned with problems of the meaning carried in messages. Psychoanalytic interventions represent an adjustable spoken input intentionally selected to resonate with a set of particular meanings in the patient's structural code. In contrast, communication engineers are concerned with a purely mathematical theory of information which is concerned not with the meaning-content of signs or symbols carrying information but only with the frequency of their occurrence. The probabilities spoken about in communication theory are these frequencies or numerical estimates of these frequencies.

According to Weaver [13] there are three levels of communication problems:

1. How accurately can symbols be transmitted? (A technical problem.)

2. How precisely do symbols convey desired meanings? (A meaning or semantic problem.)

3. How effectively does the received meaning effect conduct in some desired way? (An effectiveness problem.)

The mathematical theory of information applies only to (1), the technical problem. A psychoanalytic theory of information would be primarily interested in (2) and (3). The information exchange between patient and analyst is directed by a goal. The patient conveys information to the analyst, hoping that from it the analyst can evaluate the disturbance; in return, the analyst conveys information to the patient with the intent to modify the disturbance. For a general account of human communication see Cherry. [14]

I have summarized some contributions from five disciplines which have relevance for psychoanalysis as a science. Psychoanalysis belongs on the integrative scale of sciences in the domain of persons. Let us now turn to the field of psychoanalysis itself and consider three general problem areas. Realizing their limitations, I will follow the traditional medical divisions of psychoanalysis into problem areas of psychology, pathology, and treatment. First let us consider logico-theoretical work in these areas.

Psychoanalysis as Science

THEORY CONSTRUCTION

An ideal scientific theory represents a hypothetico-deductive system made up of theoretical statements linked to empirical statements through rules of inference. To improve the theory requires not only empirical work but also theory work aimed at clarifying, defining, explicating, systematizing, and sharpening theoretical constructs. Logical attempts must be made to weed out inconsistencies, contradictions, and other errors of inference. For instance, we cannot accept two incompatible answers to the same question and we must not confuse theorems with their converse.

These armchair thought-operations are just as important for a science as the accretion of data. And they are particularly important in a science like psychoanalysis which is struggling to move beyond a descriptive stage. To quote Freud:

We have often heard it maintained that sciences should be built up on clear and sharply defined basic concepts. In actual fact no science, not even the most exact, begins with such definitions. The true beginning of scientific activity consists rather in describing phenomena and then in proceeding to group, classify and correlate them. Even at the stage of description it is not possible to avoid applying certain abstract ideas to the material in hand, ideas derived from somewhere or other but certainly not from the new observations alone. Such ideas—which will later become the basic concepts of the science—are still more indispensable as the material is further worked over. . . . It is only after more thorough investigation of the field of observation that we are able to formulate its basic scientific concepts with increased precision, and progressively so to modify them that they become service-able and consistent over a wide area. Then, indeed, the time may have come to confine them in definitions.[15]

However these definitions must be flexible, open to emenda-tion and even discard if necessary.

One dislikes the thought of abandoning observation for barren theoretical controversy, but nevertheless one must not shirk an attempt at clarification. It is true that notions such as that of an ego-libido, an energy of the ego-instincts, and so on, are neither particularly easy to grasp, nor sufficiently rich in content; a speculative theory of the relations in question would begin by seeking to obtain a sharply defined concept as its basis. But I am of the opinion that that is just the difference between a specula-tive theory and a science erected on empirical interpretation. The latter will not envy speculation its privilege of having a smooth, logically unassailable foundation, but will gladly content itself with nebulous, scarcely imaginable basic concepts which it hopes to apprehend more clearly in the course of its development, or which it is even prepared to replace by others. For these ideas are not the foundation of science upon which everything rests: that foundation is observation alone. They are not the bottom but the top of the whole structure, and they can be replaced and dis-carded without damaging it.[16]

Thus far no one has systematized all of psychoanalytic theory and perhaps it is not ready for it. To axiomatize a theory one has to list the basic irreducible assumptions from which all others can be deduced. The list that follows is not an attempt at axiomatization. It is merely a summary of theoretical constructs in three problem areas which require further research efforts. Some of these constructs have become established while others have not; some overlap and many are derivable from the others. They all require further explication and theoretical research in relating constructs to observables and constructs to other constructs. In theoretical work we must examine and question each one of our propositions carefully for its consistency, completeness, justification, and applicability.

PSYCHOANALYTIC PSYCHOLOGY

A large number of psychoanalytic hypotheses belong to the area of healthy or ideal psychic functioning. They attempt to solve problems involved in explaining the organization of those intrapsychic operations which determine general human behavior.

Structure. Structure in psychoanalysis refers to the event structure of time-invariant functions and not to material space-occupying structure. We conceive of models which attempt to portray the interrelation of these enduring functions. Models describe a psychic apparatus as consisting of structural systems operating according to different principles but organized to interact harmoniously in generating behavior patterns. Models can be pictorialized as flow diagrams, directed graphs, or geometric manifolds.

Cathexis. When structural systems operate they are assumed to transmit information in the form of messages and to have varying degrees of activity. To conceptualize the energic form of messages and variations in activity we utilize the energy construct of cathexis.

Instinctual Drive. Psychoanalysis assumes certain inborn sets of instructions present in the material structure of the brain and appearing in the event structure of the psychic apparatus. The information content of these sets refers to specific actions toward specific objects in the external world. The inborn sets have an activating somatic source which determines a discharge threshold and external-world stimulus-configurations which, depending on thresholds, activate discharge of drive messages impelling, with varying intensities, actions toward objects. We also conceive of a variety of behavioral modes to which drive messages contribute and a maturational sequence of critical stages in which certain drives become active while others are attenuated.

Dynamics. We conceive of behavior patterns as motivated by impulses of both drive and stored-experiential origin. Motivating impulses may have the quality of consciousness-preconsciousness, or they may be unconscious. Conflicts between impulses are regulated in healthy functioning without the use of defense mechanisms.

Character. Habitual ways of integrating the demands of motivating impulses and demands of the external environment we conceive as character. In pathologic character, typical defenses are repeatedly used for regulating conflict.

Genetic Process. We have a number of hypotheses about maturation and development of the child into an adult person with a certain character. For example, the life history of a person's relations with significant other persons would represent one important aspect of the genetic process.

Dreams. Many of the above constructs are utilized in our understanding of dreams. But we also use a group of hypotheses relevant to the special process of dreaming, such as dream-work and its transformation principles.

PSYCHOANALYTIC PATHOLOGY

It will help us here if we speak of pathologic states in persons rather than of pathologic persons. Every person has some degree of malfunction, whether it be dental caries or repressed experiences. One of the confusions around the term "normal" stems from its use in the sense of "common" and its use in the sense of "healthy." It is common for persons to employ repression as a defense mechanism, but it is not healthy.

"Healthy" means that intrapsychic components are integrated in a network whose contents are available and retrievable for rational decisions of the secondary process and accessible to modification by experience. Defenses are by definition pathological since first, they operate to deny, distort, or falsify intrapsychic representations of reality, second, they cut off intrapsychic components from modification by experience, and third, they result in repetitively inappropriate patterns of behavior. Defenses represent a way the psychic apparatus can damage itself in its reparative attempts. Losing information, for example, through repression, may be strain-reducing but error-inducing, adjustive but maladaptive.

Pathogenic conflict. When a conflict is resolved through the use of defense mechanisms, pathologic states result. They include neurotic symptoms and pathologic character traits. A great variety of concepts have been used to delineate particular symptoms and particular traits.

The early conceptions of psychoanalytic psychopathologists we now realize to be oversimplifications. Today it is considered futile to attempt to link a single adult symptom with a single infantile trauma, with any single experience, or with a single dynamism. Neurotic symptoms are equifinial—that is, the same symptom can arise as an end from a variety of means. Nor is there always a one-to-one correspondence between a particular symptom and a particular kind of conflict. Pathological states are much more complex in their origin than had first been thought.

Our emphasis now in pathology is on character traits rather than on symptoms. Symptoms are viewed as the outcome of a decompensatory failure of pathologic character traits. The character constrictions and distortions maintained by unconscious infantile fantasies or beliefs arising from childhood experience constitute a focus of current psychoanalytic interest.

Psychotic States. Various concepts of psychotic states have been formulated but they are still burdened by a belief that such a condition as schizophrenia really exists. Rebels and revolutionaries in the neuroses, psychoanalysts have timidly accepted the traditional nosology of psychiatry for psychoses and have become lost in a misapplied logic for a nonexistent disorder (Szasz).[17]

Psychoanalysis as Science

PSYCHOANALYTIC TREATMENT

In the clinical analytic situation we observe at close hand the effect of person on person under specific and systematic conditions. Observable changes take place in patients' characters and behaviors. To justify our technology we have a series of concepts which, although eminently useful, are still crude and unsatisfying in their explanatory power. The main concepts refer to the analytic situation, free-association, resistance, intervention, transference, and working-through.

Analytic Situation. Patient and analyst contract to meet regularly, privately, and frequently over long periods of time. Some of the effects of treatment may be due to the nature of the analytic situation in which an analyst imposes rules on himself in order *not* to do certain things.

Free Association. We assume that to maximize our understanding of and influence over a patient's intrapsychic processes, he must describe to us in detail the conscious contents of self-observation.

Resistance. The expected optimum of free association is interfered with by resistances indicating the operation of defenses which in turn indicate an area of pathogenic conflict.

Intervention. An analyst selects certain messages to transmit to a patient with the intention of bringing about beneficial changes in the patient's psychic functioning. We believe interpretation to be the most effective informational input, but there are so many interacting processes in psychoanalytic

[71]

treatment that no one yet knows which ingredients of the shotgun prescription are active and which are inert.

Transference. In the course of treatment the patient develops nonrational reactions to the analyst which are connected to childhood reactions to parents. They become first-hand examples of nonrational modes suitable for interpretation.

Working Through. The adult psychic apparatus is highly stable to informational input. Selective inputs must be repeatedly run through a patient's structural code over long stretches of time before the code changes in a durable way. Over and over, in a variety of contexts, the same message inputs must be introduced by the analyst and assimilated by the patient.

I have listed the main theoretical constructs of psychoanalysis in three problem areas of psychology, pathology, and treatment. They have been the concern of psychoanalytic investigation to date and will undoubtedly continue to concern us. We need a more rigorous application of appropriate scientific methods in all of these areas. They are open to scientific inquiry because decidable questions can be formulated in them. We can subject these hypotheses to some sort of empirical test and decide whether or not, and within what limits, the hypotheses are correct.

In contrast, there have been areas entered by psychoanalysis in which decidable questions cannot logically be formulated. There are many pseudo-problems, as far as science is concerned, and to expend efforts over them is to waste our scientific energies. Of necessity this is a personal opinion.

Psychoanalysis as Science

Often enough in the history of science just when the elders decide that some idea is worthless or that some problem is theoretically unsolvable, upstarts appear to demonstrate that just the opposite holds. (Johannes Müller carefully explained why the rate of transmission of the nerve impulse could never be measured, whereupon Helmholtz measured it.) Each generation of analysts decides what it is interested in and what it will believe. Accepting the penalty of being proved wrong, I believe the following questions are undecidable and should be considered as beyond the range of scientific psychoanalysis, although they may occupy other sorts of psychoanalytic interest.

UNDECIDABLE QUESTIONS

I will group those questions I consider unpromising for scientific research in four categories.

Questions Regarding Behavior of Paleolithic Man: Assertions about complex patterns of human behavior before written records require such a high level of inference from so little evidence that they can only be considered speculations. Problems like Darwin's primal horde (even Freud called it a scientific myth), man's initial feelings about fire, the first religious beliefs, and the origin of the incest taboo are fun to think about and write essays about. But the hypotheses cannot be refuted in principle and there is no way of coming to a yes or no decision about them.

Questions Regarding Phylogenetic Memories. The hypotheses that assert that somehow the experience of our individual ancestors became coded in genes and transmitted to their offspring are not accessible to decision as they now stand, and the evidence from animal biology tends to be against them. We do know that genes can carry highly complex instructions and it is not too implausible to believe that some of them may include inheritable information. Suitable experiments could be carried out to decide the question were it not for society's strong moral objections to depriving infants of direct human contact. Without these experiments the hypotheses remain as speculative ideas.

Questions Regarding Biographies of Great Men. Psychoanalytic studies of Moses, Leonardo, Poe, and Shakespeare are fascinating and entertaining. But they are not science; they belong to art, literature, or history. Some will argue that history is a science, since it offers evidence for hypotheses and comes to conclusions on the basis of evidence. Thus history could be compared to the sciences of geology or paleontology. The counterargument insists that the evidence is too unreliable to test hypotheses and too insufficient to establish general conclusions. Science is interested in useful generalizations about a class. An individual biography may illustrate some generalization arrived at through other evidence. Psychoanalysts are hero worshippers with verbal skills, therefore they will continue to make biographical studies. These idiographic, rather than nomothetic, efforts may result in literature but not in science. When art and science accost the same questions they have quite different criteria for acceptable answers.

Psychoanalysis as Science

Questions Regarding Mass Behavior. When psychoanalysts make public assertions about causes of war, of economic depression, of overpopulation and other social discontents, these should be taken not as sound scientific statements but just as sound. We are free to offer interpretations about entire nations or trade barriers but we should not delude ourselves as to their truth status. Nor should we attempt to endow such factually insouciant generalizations with the dignity of science because of our status as experts on human behavior. Pronouncements about international politics by psychoanalysts belong to the area of ordinary everyday mistakes rather than that of scientific mistakes.

These four categories of undecidable questions represent topics which we can neglect. If an investigator wishes to add to knowledge, he must channel his energies into problem areas in which the questions are accessible and there is some probability of discoverable answers. From these problem areas he must make a judicious and Spartan selection of problems around which he can generate bright ideas testable by scientific methods. Assuming he follows this advice, what scientific methods will a psychoanalytic investigator find most suitable and appropriate for his subject matter?

NOTES

1. These two quotations are from S. Freud, "A Philosophy of Life," *New Introductory Lectures* (London: Hogarth Press, 1946).

2. Justifiable criticisms are discussed in detail in A. E. Ellis, "An Introduction to the Principles of Scientific Psychoanalysis," *Genetic Psychology Monographs,* 41 (1950), 147-212; and C. Hall and G. Lindzey, *Theories of Personality* (New York: John Wiley & Sons, 1957).

3. Important new facts about the dream process can be found in the work of W. Dement and N. Kleitman, "The Relation of Eye Movements During Sleep to Dream Activity," *Journal of Experimental Psychology,* 53 (1957), 339-346.

4. Neurophysiologists worth keeping track of are H. W. Magoun, "The Ascending Reticular System and Wakefulness," in *Brain Mechanisms and Consciousness* (Springfield, Ill.: Charles C Thomas, 1954); P. McLean, "The Limbic System with Respect to Self-Preservation and the Preservation of the Species," *Journal of Nervous & Mental Disease,* 127 (1958), 1-11; R. Gerard, "The Biological Roots of Psychiatry," *American Journal of Psychiatry,* 112 (1955), 81-90.

5. After psychology separated itself from deductive philosophy (Kant even testified in court as a psychiatrist), philosophers became neglected. But some of them still have arresting ideas for us to consider—for example, H. Feigl, "The Mental and the Physical," in *Minnesota Studies in the Philosophy of Science,* (Minneapolis, Minn.: University of Minnesota Press, 1958), Vol. II, pp. 370-497.

6. J. Bowlby, "The Nature of the Child's Tie to His Mother," *International Journal of Psychoanalysis,* 39 (1958), 1-24; R.

Fletcher, *Instinct in Man* (New York: International Universities Press, 1957); C. Schiller, *Instinctive Behavior* (New York: International Universities Press, 1957).

7. L. Festinger, *Theory of Cognitive Dissonance* (Evanston, Ill.: Row, Peterson & Co., 1957).

8. In the past, psychology has been precise about things that do not matter much, whereas psychoanalysis has been sloppy about things that matter a great deal. A welcome rapprochement occurs in F. Heider, *The Psychology of Interpersonal Relations* (New York: John Wiley & Sons, 1958).

9. Do not be misled by the title. The book is invaluable for all investigators in human behavior. G. Lindzey (Ed.), *Handbook of Social Psychology* (Cambridge: Addison-Wesley, Inc., 1954).

10. With a superb twenty-five page bibliography: W. LaBarre, "The Influence of Freud on Anthropology," *American Imago,* 15 (1958), 275-328.

11. C. Kluckhohn, "Universal Categories of Culture," in A. L. Kroeber (Ed.), *Anthropology Today* (Chicago: University of Chicago Press, 1953).

12. D. M. Schneider, Attempts to Account for the Incest Taboo. Unpublished paper.

13. The mathematical sections of this classic are too specialized for the psychoanalyst but Weaver's discussions are easily understood. See C. E. Shannon and W. Weaver, *The Mathematical Theory of Communication* (Urbana: University of Illinois Press, 1949).

14. The best book on the topic for nonmathematicians is C. Cherry, *On Human Communication* (New York: John Wiley & Sons, 1957).

15. S. Freud, "Instincts and Their Vicissitudes," *Standard Edition of the Collected Works* (London: The Hogarth Press, 1957), Vol. XIV, p. 117.

16. S. Freud, "On Narcissism," *Standard Edition of the Col-*

lected Works (London: The Hogarth Press, 1957), Vol. XIV, p. 77.

17. If I say that a patient is schizophrenic you should be able to infer deductively that he possesses certain attributes characteristic of members of the class identified by this label. Since this cannot be done with any degree of regularity, the clinical usefulness of the class and its label has come to an end. (See T. S. Szasz, "The Problem of Psychiatric Nosology," *American Journal of Psychiatry,* 117 (1957), 405-413.

:IV:
Research in the Analytic Situation

ANOTHER FABLE[1]

ONCE UPON A TIME there were three psychoanalysts who, after their long period of training, still retained sparks of scientific curiosity about human behavior. They had reached frontier levels of knowledge in the field and were interested in the discovery of new facts and ideas. When faced with the requirements of a scientific approach to psychoanalytic problems, they began to realize their shortcomings in this search. They became discouraged and each developed a different compensatory reaction.

The first became an Antiscientific Psychoanalyst. He felt that it was too late to educate himself as an investigator and hopeless for him to learn these new statistics. He was too old, too tired, and had too many children, dogs, wives, and cars to support. He began to doubt whether a scientific approach could be made toward psychoanalytic problems. He soon stated publicly that our data was so unique it could not be subjected to the paraphernalia of precision. It could not be measured nor experimented with. (Here he drew on a hackneyed, but mistaken, comparison with astronomy, unaware that astronomers measure and manipulate their variables in signal form and even experiment with matter obtained as meteors.) Nowadays he plays up third-ear intuition and speaks mysteriously of unknown depths. As a Jack the Science Killer, he scoffs at numbers, formulae, logic. He even asserts the primary process to be the source of true knowledge. He points out that there is more to life and people than quantities. He warns us that the uniqueness of the individual must not be lost and that we must respect the eternal mysteries (otherwise how could they remain eternal?). Instead of analysts his colleagues are annalists, religionists, existential philosophers. He turns to the humanities in his reading and perhaps will become a scholar of history, biography, or art.

The second psychoanalyst also became discouraged but reacted in a different way. He became a convert to SCIENCE (he pronounces it now in capital letters). The Ultrascientific Psychoanalyst felt that what he learned in his training was merely crude, clinical folklore handed down during an oppressive apprenticeship. It was all worthless as a basis for a scientific approach. Only numbers, exactitude, and quantification offered any hope. Confounding research with someone else's technology, he rejected clinical methods and skills except as a means of earning a living. He now turns to other disciplines which have already been accepted as scientific in order to find laws and explanations. He too becomes isolated from analysts, but he feels that he must be on the right track because his new colleagues know what real science is all about.

Every fable must have its hero; we come to ours in the person of the Scientific Psychoanalyst. Discouragement over his shortcomings spurred him into efforts to correct them. He felt that gaps in his knowledge could be filled in by self-educational attempts to gain what is only human information acquirable through study. He weighed the assets of his knowledge as well and was convinced that there were special advantages to the clinical analytic situation for the study of human behavior. If clinical knowledge and experience could be supplemented by research tools appropriate to psychoanalytic problems, there awaited opportunities for new discoveries. With study he came to realize the pitfalls in blindly adopting constructs and techniques of other scientific fields. He now retains analysts as his colleagues because it is they who best know what the critical problems are and who best understand the theory of past approaches to them. To the Antiscientist he replies that research itself is not a science but as much a creative art as any artist might crave. To the Ultrascientist he replies that it is futile to withdraw to a supposedly simpler discipline, because every subject matter is discouragingly complex the more one knows about it.

Whether this fable describes three psychoanalysts or just one in different phases of development, the reactions are observable and understandable. An analyst need not become Anti- or Ultra- if he can feel some respect for his knowledge and if he can be helped in directing it into scientific types of inquiry. Previously we spoke of a scientist as a person who makes observations and/or experiments to collect data relevant to a hypothesis about a problem in order to decide whether or not the hypothesis is correct. The heart of all this is the problem and the hypothesis, since these, not statistics, initiate inquiry. To grasp what problem is both essential and answerable and to guess at likely and testable hypotheses about it require prior knowledge of a field. It is here that clinical psychoanalytic knowledge and experience are so invaluable. A boy of eighteen can make discoveries in physics or mathematics but not in psychoanalysis. To get to the frontiers of research in psychoanalysis requires years of study, especially in order to master theory. For it is theory, much more than observation, which suggests interesting questions suitable for testing.

THE CLINICAL ANALYTIC SITUATION

An analyst can add to the accumulation of knowledge simply but powerfully by making systematic inquiries into those observations available to him. What are his available observations? Mainly they consist of events taking place in the clinical analytic situation. Of course, an analyst can observe human behavior in all sorts of situations in life, from psychiatric wards to newspaper stories to play with his children. But his chief opportunity for systematic, recorded, and controlled observation leading to maximum information occurs in the clinical analytic situation.

Verbal definitions being quite arbitrary, there are many ways of defining what is psychoanalytic research. A broad definition might include any observations of human behavior ordered by psychoanalytic concepts. But here I will use a restricted definition of psychoanalytic research to mean research concerning a specific subject-matter, methods of observation and methods of operation. The subject-matter consists of inclusive spoken descriptions of self-observation by persons in the analytic situation. The method of observation involves listening, introspection and empathy as the analyst observes himself identifying with descriptions of another person's self-observation. The method of operation by the analyst consists of setting up an analytic situation and using spoken interventions guided by clinico-theoretical principles. Central to these three dimensions is the analytic situation.

Our best fact-finding, data-collecting, and hypothesis-testing chances lie in this situation which is standardized, repeatable, and reproducible by multiple observers. It provides access to data (inclusive self-descriptions) not otherwise collectable; it is close enough to real-life situations to make reliable generalizations about human behavior; it is simplified enough to study a few variables at a time; and it permits both naturalistic and experimental observation. We can gather large amounts of data from individuals and observe variations over long periods of time. In fact, analysts should challenge other students of human behavior to set up as good a situation for the scientific study of persons. It may be that the importance of psychoanalysis for human endeavor lies not in its method of treating disease (its results in the medical sense of therapy are thus far unimpressive) but in its method of investigating behavior in a controllable way.

Observed facts are a function of the method of observation. Since most psychoanalytic observation takes place in the clinical situation, let us now describe this situation and a scientific strategy appropriate to it. We can divide what we believe are the essential variables into five groups as follows:

Setting. Events of the clinical analytic situation take place in a room or office which is much the same everywhere. It contains a couch with a chair behind it, a desk, a few chairs, books, pictures, etc. The decor and arrangement of the furniture remain constant for months and years. The closed door has a sign function of a privacy, even an intimacy, brooking no interruptions.

Persons. The analyst has the status of a professional expert who provides certain services and the patient has the status of a person willing to purchase these services. They have had no previous social relationship and none develops during the analysis. Analyst and patient usually share the interests and folkways of the upper-middle and lower-upper classes.

Collaboration. Their working relation represents a task-directed collaboration. The patient attempts to describe everything resulting from self-observation while the analyst attempts to sustain a steady, objective neutrality toward what he hears and sees. There is a mutual trust in an implied contract that the patient will describe everything in consciousness while the analyst will keep this to himself and not use it against the patient. Frankness is exchanged for discretion. The patient talks about everything to the analyst, the analyst talks only about the patient to the patient.

Communication. The patient communicates in the form of inclusive description of self-observation during free association. The analyst's communications take the form of interventions (including use of silence as a message in certain contexts). The communications represent a continuously interacting exchange in which the configuration of the moment is determined by what has gone on before and what can be anticipated in the near future.

Time. The length of the session, its frequency per week, its number per year, and the number of years represent important variables. The exchange of communications between the persons collaborating in this setting must continue over long periods of time before desired modifications take place in the patient.

From clinical experience we believe these groups make up variables essential to the kinds of observations we make in the analytic situation. There has been little systematic work done on manipulating these variables to see whether they really are essential, or which are essential while others are irrelevant. Perhaps other variables we have not even considered may turn out to be the important ones. The problem of how to translate the poetry of the analytic situation into the prose of science awaits an experimental translator.

COMMUNICANT OBSERVATION

Our fact-finding situation involves processes characteristic of observation in the domain of persons. These processes differ in important respects from observation in the domain of things. The most important contrast is reflected in participant and communicant observation.

Observation in the domain of things, at least of large-scale things, is characterized by a negligible effect of an observer on the thing. When we observe a large-scale thing such as a planet or a palace, we do in fact effect it slightly, but the effect is so small that we can ignore it and for practical purposes say the observer has no effect on the observed. However, in the instance of small-scale things, such as electrons, the effect of observation is very great. Shining a light on an electron to observe it disturbs its position violently. When you ask an electron, "Where are you?" the effort of replying moves the electron so much that its answer is automatically invalidated. Persons are large-scale things in the world, but when they are observed by other persons and are aware of it, they can behave like electrons.

In the domain of persons, observer and observed observe one another observing. A person aware of being observed observes in return. So the first characteristic of participant observation is that observer and observed belong to the same classes. Such crisscrossing awarenesses and simultaneous class membership introduce problems not found when a person observes things. The second characteristic is that persons in proximity to one another tend to communicate. An observed person aware of being observed attempts intentionally to send signs and signals to his observer. Persons have intentions and they strive to reach out toward one another with signs and messages; this fact makes them an observed different from a glacier or a flatiron.

A third characteristic of observed persons is that they not only observe and make inferences in return but they can make inferences about inferences. They construct hypotheses about the construction of hypotheses. These meta-level capacities are unique to persons as an observed in nature.

A final property of importance for the domain of persons concerns confirmations by self-observation. As the most privileged observer of himself, a person can confirm statements about himself made to him by another person. These may be weak confirmations compared to metrical measurements in the domain of things. But, compared to crude estimates of motivations in nonhuman animals, they are powerful aids in testing inferences about behavior.

There is one other feature important for observation in the analytic situation: the analyst, an observer, also observes himself. I am not referring to the type of self-observation inherent in all observation. An astronomer does not actually observe a something way out there when he observes a red planet. He observes something in himself which represents the combination of signals from a planet and his stored information, the computational end-product being called a percept. When I refer to the analyst's self-observation I mean not only his percepts of the patient and his decipherings of the patient's messages but also his private thoughts and feelings about himself. The potentials of an analyst's self-observation as a source of working hypotheses are still underestimated. For example, much of what is termed "understanding" the patient derives from an analyst's hunting through empathic echo-responses in himself and matching them with his percepts of the patient. Systematic self-observation by analysts offers promise of new information about mental life. Introspection, once disparaged as unreliably subjective, is now beginning to be recognized even by operationalists as a type of observation and hence a legitimate source of data.

Believing that observation in the analytic situation can lead to valuable scientific information about human behavior, how would an analyst proceed to carry out an empirical research inquiry using this observational opportunity? Let me briefly state what a working scientist does:

1. He makes observations in certain situations.

2. He searches for regularities in the observations.

3. He formulates principles giving a causal explanation of the regularities.

We have discussed (1) and every analyst is familiar with the kinds of observations made in the analytic situation. Hence we come to (2), the regularities of observation. We cannot formulate dependable explanatory principles until we have sorted out some empirical regularity.

Research in the Analytic Situation

REGULARITIES IN ANALYTIC OBSERVATION

In making observations we come to recognize that property A is often found associated with property B or that event A and event B recur in the same order. We discover that certain facts go together while others do not. We classify facts on the basis of similarities, differences, and recurrences. Once we suspect (or hope for) the presence of a regularity, we try to establish how regular it is. Finally we attempt to formulate a causal basis for the regularities observed.

Applying these steps to the analytic situation, let us see how analysts discovered regularities by searching for correlations and concomitant variations. Here are some familiar examples.

Observing inclusive self-descriptions of persons in the analytic situation, Freud noticed three features, a triad of character traits, recurrently found together in the same person. The traits were orderliness, stubbornness, and stinginess. Subsequently this correlation has been confirmed by various psychological tests. There is some surprise to the correlation since, in our culture, orderliness is considered a desirable trait whereas stubbornness and stinginess are not. The first step in discovery of regularity is to recognize a cluster whose items are significantly related. The next step is to hazard an explanation of the regularity. Freud stated that this triad of properties developed in persons who had great infantile pleasure in anal sensations. His explanation involves still another correlation, this one of the causal, *If A, then B* type.

The causal correlation, while plausible, has not yet been confirmed.

Through clinical observation a correlation has been noted between the symptom of impotence in men and their unconscious belief in coitus as a dangerous castration threat. Upon modification of this belief, the impotence disappears. From this concomitant variation, a causal correlation has been formulated which is now a useful part of every analyst's knowledge.

Naturalistic observation led to the correlations of a specific type of love-object choice made by certain men. Men were observed who described four conditions necessary for their falling in love. When these conditions were met by an actual woman, these men experienced intense love. The conditions were: (1) The woman must belong to another man; (2) She must have an unvirtuous reputation, having many flirtations or lovers of whom the man is extremely jealous while not feeling jealous of her husband or fiancé; (3) The woman must be highly overevaluated, and she may be one of a long series of repeated passionate attachments; (4) The man feels a need to protect and rescue her, otherwise she will lose all respectability and rapidly sink to the level of prostitute. The first two of these conditions involve properties of the loved woman while the second two concern his behavior toward her.

For Freud's explanation of these correlations I would refer you to his paper on the subject.[2]

It was one of Freud's talents to see correlations in persons and in self-descriptions where others saw nothing. Again, it is worth comment that he noted facts appearing together which seem antithetical, disparate. They have a surprise value for us since they do not make sense at first. We have certain expectations for human behavior and the combination of jealousy toward lovers but not toward a husband strikes us as unintelligible since these properties seem so incompatible. But there they stand, easily observable now that they have been pointed out.

To remind us that clinical naturalistic observation has its pitfalls, let us remember Freud's erroneous etiological correlation between the presence of syphilis in the male parent and the occurrence of childhood neurosis. Freud had observed cases of neurosis in which the father had syphilis. But syphilis was not a rare disease in those days. If he had kept track of the negative instances, he might not have been misled, since this is a type of correlation readily disconfirmable by simple enumeration.

Finally, an example of a correlation occurring during the course of psychoanalytic treatment: Clinically we can observe a correlation between the sudden rise of an intercurrent resistance and the development of a transference reaction.

These are examples of correlations typical for the analytic situation. We try to establish through observation whether certain informational facts or observable properties actually hang together, at first in one person and eventually in a class of persons. If they do, then we have come across a regularity, a stable invariant which merits the next step of causal explanation.

TYPES OF CORRELATION

Each investigator has his own way of searching for and noting correlations. What follows is a way of classifying recurrent correlations possible in the analytic situation. The examples given range from slight to unimportant, since unfortunately one can be clearest about trivia.

1. Correlations between one action of the patient and another; for example, before lying on the couch, some men regularly take off their coats.

2. Correlations between specific output messages, meaning-bearing statements from the patient, and his actions; for example, when persons express shame they shield their eyes by rubbing their forehead between thumb and forefinger.

3. Correlations between a specific output message and a type of person; for example, only women report the childhood belief that kissing leads to impregnation.

4. Correlations between specific output messages and other specific output messages; for example, when a woman describes a bad period of overeating and untidiness during menstruation she will subsequently describe the remainder of a cycle as a good period of dieting and house-cleaning.

5. Correlations between an action by the analyst and an action by the patient; for example, when the analyst shifts in his chair, the patient in a resistant state changes his position on the couch.

6. Correlations between a selected input message by the analyst and subsequent output messages from the patient;

for example, an interpretation by the analyst reinforces a topic in the patient's sequent associations.

7. Correlations between output messages from the patient and messages occurring within the analyst about himself; for example, when a patient reports significant events of his childhood, an analyst envisages his own childhood.

In searching for recurrent correlations in the analytic situation we act as both naturalistic and experimental observers. Observing naturalistically we note that when we find *A*, we also find *B*. Observing experimentally we note that when we create *A* (by intervening technically), we produce *B* (an alteration in free association). Also we observe nature's experiments inasmuch as patients report that when *A* occurred in their lives, it was followed by *B*. The repeated recurrence of such *A-B* sequences provides the necessary temporal contiguities for causal explanation.

PROBABILITY THEORY

Earlier, two kinds of causal laws were described. The first took the form *If A, then always B*. As an exceptionless causal correlation, it represents a strict causal law. The second took the form *If A, then B in some regular percentage of cases*. This represents a probability causal law allowing for exceptions to the causal correlation.

Naturalistic and experimental observation in the analytic situation lead to the formulation of probability causal laws. Since many analysts are unfamiliar with probability theory as one of the suitable mathematical frameworks for psycho-analytic inquiry, let us diverge for a moment.

A branch of mathematics, probability theory began in the sixteenth and seventeenth centuries with attempts, at first by Cardano and later by Pascal and Fermat, to aid the solution of gambling problems in dice and cards. These games are still used today to illustrate ideas in probability theory (because we see life and the future as a gamble?) although drawing marbles from an urn now runs them a close second (to add another gambling metaphor). Cards, dice, and marbles allow us to be precise about simple things in very restricted contexts. When it comes to human behavior, however, we often find that the games are unfair; the dice are loaded, the cards sticky, and persons do not always follow the rules, making tenuous the equiprobable assumptions inherent to classical probability theory.

Among the experts there is still no consensus as to what probability is. Mathematicians, philosophers, and scientists present varying interpretations. Also, there are some annoying circularities involved. To talk about probability we have to assume randomness, but to talk about randomness we must assume probability.

Today there are roughly two interpretations of probability as represented by two kinds of probability statements.[3]

Statistical Statements. For example, statements such as "The probability of a head in tossing a normal coin is $1/2$." If we toss a coin 100 times and get 47 heads, 53 tails, the quotient $\dfrac{\text{heads}}{\text{tosses}} = \dfrac{47}{100}$ is called the relative frequency of heads. As the heads and tosses become larger the quotient approaches a limiting value of 1/2. This limiting value is taken as a measure of the probability of heads. Under the statistical or frequentist view, probability means the limiting value of the relative frequency of an event in a long sequence of trials (a rub lies in the term "long," for in the truly long run we are dead). Since something is counted and a computation made, the calculus of probabilities is applicable.

Degree of Confirmation Statements. Examples here would be statements such as "It is probable that Shakespeare wrote those plays," or "It is improbable that it will rain today," or "The theory of evolution is more probable than the theory of special creation." To these statements it is difficult to give a numerical measure and to apply the calculus of probabilities. We depend on the weight of evidence which tends to confirm or disconfirm. The weight of evidence is a function not only of the number of positive instances but also of kinds of instances and of the relative number of each kind.

These two types of statements represent the dualistic interpretation of probability theory. There is another interpretation termed the "subjectivistic," or neoclassical, which is opposed to any frequentist view.[4] Although some probability-theorists consider it naive, empirical scientists use a relative frequency definition of probability since they find it useful. We can trust mathematicians to argue this out and ourselves turn now to how probability theory can be used as an aid in evaluating correlations in the analytic situation. We can use it to test our hypotheses about regularities and about causal explanations of these regularities.

AN ILLUSTRATIVE EXAMPLE

Suppose that in the analytic situation we have observed several women who report that as little girls they believed a woman could become pregnant from kissing a man.

We might wonder about generalizations such as "Is this belief limited to women?" or "Did all women patients believe this as little girls?" or "Did all women believe this?" This small group of women might be considered to represent a sample of a variety of total populations.

Let the first circle in the left-hand rectangle in Figure 1 represent the class of all women patients, the second circle the class of all ideas of an oral impregnation belief; in the right-hand rectangle we have a combination of the two.

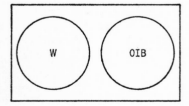 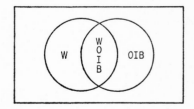

Figure 1

The sum $W + OIB$ would represent the union of the two classes. The negation W, not OIB, would represent the difference between them, while $WOIB$ in the second rectangle is the product or intersection of the two classes. (Incidentally, these three operations form the basis of set theory, or algebra of classes, another branch of mathematics which may also have applications in psychoanalysis.)

We are interested in the class *WOIB*, a subclass of both *W* and *OIB*. We have observed some members of the class *WOIB*, women patients with an oral impregnation belief. What conclusions can we make about a whole class on the basis of drawing a sample from it? Can we conclude that all oral impregnation beliefs occur in women; that is, the

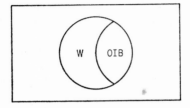

Figure 2

class *OIB* is included in the class women? (See Figure 2.) Or can we conclude that all women patients have oral impregnation beliefs; that is, the class of women is included

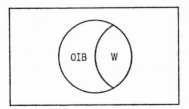

Figure 3

in the class of oral impregnation beliefs? (Figure 3.) The steps involved in our inquiry would run as follows:

An Introduction to Psychoanalytic Research

1. We wonder whether our correlation represents a true regularity. Perhaps it is a "chance" observation. Suppose we had a well-shaken urn of assorted marbles, known to be of different sizes and colors. We draw five marbles one at a time and they are all the same size and all black. Could we generalize that probably all the marbles this size are black? Our observation of five similar marbles might be due to randomness, to unknown variables in drawing the sample. The next marble we draw might be of the same size but a different color, or black but of a different size. Fortunately, we have a statistical way of deciding whether outcomes are due to random factors or whether they represent a true regularity.

2. Let us start with the hypothesis that what we have observed *is* due to random factors in selection. We start with what we do not really want to believe in order to disprove it. This hypothesis is termed the null hypothesis, the hypothesis of no differences. It would assert, for example, that men as well as women had oral impregnation beliefs or that white as well as black marbles were of a certain size. The null hypothesis, H_0, is formulated in order to be *rejected* by the facts of observation. If we can reject it, then we feel safer about an alternative hypothesis, H_1, which asserts there are true differences. Failure to reject H_0 of course does not establish it as true.

3. We choose an appropriate statistical test for testing H_0. By appropriate we mean (a) a test whose model most closely approximates the conditions of the inquiry, (b) a test whose measurement requirement is met by the measures used in the inquiry. To elaborate:

[98]

a) The tests suitable for psychoanalytic research are small-sample, or nonparametric, tests. The advantages of these tests are that they are distribution-free (they do not assume the scores come from a normally distributed population), their computations are simple and easily learned, and their scores do not have to be exact in the numerical sense but can be simply rank orders.

b) To measure is to assign numbers or other symbols to observations in accordance with some rule. The rules and resulting measurement scales in science are summarized as follows:

(1) Nominal scale. A symbol or number is used to classify a person, an attribute, or a class. The symbols are labels which identify and classify. For example, the letter p can stand for a diagnostic class such as "paranoid," or certain numbers can represent a class of football players with guards numbered by the 60's and tackles by the 70's. The difference in the numbers does not indicate that tackles are worth more than guards. The numbers mean only that all players numbered in the 60's are equivalent in that they are all members of the class guards. The basic empirical operations in the nominal scale are determinations of equality. Appropriate statistical tests are binomial and chi-square tests which focus on the frequencies in classes as determined by simple enumeration. The most common measure of correlation for nominal data is the contingency coefficient.

(2) Ordinal scale. Given a nominal scale, the members of a class or items in a category can be ranked. For example one member of the class paranoid can be said to be more paranoid than another. The symbol $>$ is used to represent the rank of more, greater, higher than, etc. This scale reflects the rank order of items and its basic empirical operations are determinations of greater or less. Suitable tests are correlation coefficients based on rankings such as Spearman's *rho*.

(3) Interval scale. Given an ordinal scale, when the distances between any two numbers is known, we obtain an equal-interval scale. The numbers reflect differences among items and the basic empirical operations are determinations of differences or intervals. The zero point on the scale is arbitrary, as for example on a temperature scale. Suitable statistical tests are parametric tests, arithmetic means, and the Pearson product-moment correlation.

(4) Ratio scale. Given an interval scale, when a true zero point is known, a ratio scale results. It reflects ratios among items and its basic empirical operations are determinations of equality or ratios. For example, weight is measured on a ratio scale. Suitable tests are the parametric tests.

In the person sciences it is the nominal and ordinal levels of measurement which are usually achieved. Psychoanalysts are sometimes publicly embarassed by the question "Can you measure it?" Thinking that measurement means only interval or ratio determinations, they reply, "No," and then try nobly to defend the hopeless position that they observe events which cannot be measured. If anything can be said to exist, it can be measured, at least on a nominal scale. While comparatively weak, a nominal scale is a prerequisite for all other scales. When we deputize numbers or symbols to represent observations in psychoanalysis we are measuring, whether we realize it or not. But it should help us to realize it.

4. In the next step, we choose a level of significance. If a statistical test gives a value whose probability of occurrence under H_0 is less than some small probability called "level of significance," we reject H_0 and accept H_1. Common values of this small probability are .05 and .01. They mean that five out of 100 times or once out of 100 times, the observed outcome could be due to random factors. This value is so small that, instead of saying we have observed a rare chance occurrence, we are willing to admit that something other than chance is operating. The level of significance gives the probability of mistakenly *rejecting* H_0 and this probability is termed the Type I error. The Type II error is mistakenly to *accept* H_0 when it is in fact false. To reduce both errors we try to raise the number of cases in the sample. (All of this is described and explained far better in Siegel.[5])

To illustrate, let us take our example. Suppose we have observed only five women in the analytic situation, but all of them reported the oral impregnation belief. Is this a statistically significant observation? The data are on a nominal scale, with five cases in the class of women with an oral belief and zero cases of women without such a belief. Using the binomial test which is suitable for data falling in two classes, we find that the probability of H_0 being true is .03. If we have selected the .05 level of significance, then our findings justify rejecting H_0. However, suppose we observed six women in the analytic situation, finding in one of them no evidence of such a belief. Then the probability under H_0 is .10, and since it is above our .05 level of significance we have just failed to reject H_0. The advantages of having ten or twelve cases instead of five or six are that exceptions can occur with the distribution remaining significant. For instance, if ten women had the belief while two did not, the probability of H_0 being true is only .02. In fact fourteen cases with two exceptions ($p = .006$) is stronger evidence than six cases with no exceptions ($p = .016$).

SOME DRAWBACKS

Our example illustrating one use of probability theory in psychoanalysis has involved the Neyman-Pearson interpretation of probability, which utilizes a null hypothesis, one or more alternative hypotheses, a choice of level of significance, and the selection of a critical set of results which leads to rejection of the null hypothesis.

There are several limitations and disadvantages to this view. First, it is rather a negative approach assuming complete ignorance. We obtain objectivity perhaps, but at the price of wasting information. It is unrealistic to use prior knowledge only for selection of an alternative hypothesis. We have varying degrees of belief in hypotheses, and even if we cannot assign this subjective probability a numerical measure, we can partially rank order it. Second, under the Neyman-Pearson view the alternative hypothesis must be stated in advance of the collection of testing observations. Again, this is unrealistic and wasteful for the practical scientist. After collecting data he may find they may be used for some new hypothesis. In fact, there are some who claim this is an ideal procedure, since the post-collection hypothesis could not have biased the observations. But the danger of formulating a theory after data collection should be clear. The apparent regularities in the data may have arisen from chance.

Finally there exists an assumption of a random sample in this use of probability theory. Since the results are evaluated in terms of the probability that they might be due to random factors, the random factors must be given a "chance" to demonstrate their influence. In clinical work we must take what we can get, which is a group of self-selected patients. This group could be considered to be a population rather than a random sample although others might claim it has been naturally, if not artificially, randomized. In experimental work we can approach the ideal of a random sample through the use of stratification and systematic selection techniques. But again, we should not be so rigorous as to induce rigor mortis. Randomness is a function of the information possessed by an observer. Every sample is biased in some direction since some sort of order can always be attributed to it by an observer. True randomness represents an ideal or limiting notion never achieved but which is useful in empirical science. We try only to generalize from samples in which a bias is not correlated with the variables under study.

There are other uses of probability theory in the analytic situation. In listening to inclusive self-descriptions, we observe state-sequences with a continuous parameter of time. Markovian chains and other types of stochastic processes provide suitable mathematical frameworks for this kind of observation.[6] In the analytic situation we can count frequencies of events over long stretches of time and thus establish an estimate of probability as relative frequency, i.e., the ratio of the frequency of an event in a total class of events. For us probabilities are exact measures as real as the measures of weight or distance in physics.

CRUCIAL REGULARITIES

Research possibilities in the clinical situation center around the discovery of correlations which lead to the establishing of empirical regularities. We can achieve this through naturalistic and experimental observation. We must remember that the limitations of naturalistic observation lie in the fact that we cannot manipulate certain variables and hence are subject to *post hoc, ergo propter hoc* fallacies. Our experimental observations are still in crude and unsystematic forms. We are far from the experimental precision and rigor of hard laboratory sciences. There is some solace for the clinical investigator in the knowledge that a subtle type of limitation develops in those devoted exclusively to experimentation: the pure experimenter can get so concerned with careful and cautious testing of hypotheses that he runs dry of creative speculation. He then has to borrow bright ideas from others, just as academic psychology, blindly dominated by sterile experimentation in the past, now borrows psychoanalytic hypotheses for fresh viewpoints. We need a clinical situation to discover hypotheses and an experimental situation to test them. A combination of clinical approaches to find hypotheses and experimental approaches to test them should produce the maximum research yield.

Analysts sometimes feel they observe too few cases to discover regularities or to establish reliable generalizations. But, as we have seen, small-sample statistics are designed to permit statistically significant inferences with as few as five cases. More important than size of a sample is its composition. Psychoanalytic research involves hypothesis-testing rather than estimation of parameters. To test an explicit hypothesis we must set up a plan or design in which the cases used for observation represent a sample of the population the hypothesis is generalizing about. The observations collected from this sample should yield maximum information relative to the time, effort expended, and cases available.[7] Also, we should keep in mind that the individual is inherently lawful. Depending on the circumstances, a regularity discovered in only one person may be highly significant theoretically.

Another reservation often proposed is that analysts deal with persons each of whom is a unique individual like no other individual. Hence one cannot compare persons like things. This view misunderstands the logical basis of generalizing about a class. No two things in the universe are alike in all their respects. Every atom, every event is unique. When we say that atoms or persons are alike, we mean only that they are similar in certain, but not all, of their attributes. A class, about which we can generalize, consists of members possessing the same property. The members are alike only in that they share that property. Thus persons as well as things can be compared on the basis of similar properties which comprise the ingredients of regularities.

To discover recurrent correlations and regularities is our first job. But which regularities are important? To find those regularities which are crucial and highly important for a science requires a talent best, if vaguely, ascribed to the art of science. Suppose we establish that certain men take off their coats in the analytic situation? Does this say anything profound about human behavior? Suppose it is only women who believe in oral impregnation. What good is this regularity? How does it help us in psychology, pathology, or treatment? What problem is it relevant *for,* what can we do with it? Can we use it to predict or modify human beliefs?

It has been the gift of eminent scientists to grasp the relevance or importance of a regularity for some problem area in human experience. Others before Fleming noted a correlation between the presence of molds and inhibited growth of staphylococcal colonies. They considered the correlation to be both trivial and annoying. It took a Fleming to establish the correlation as a regularity and to discover penicillin in 1929. But then even he dropped the problem, and later it took a Florey to grasp the significance of penicillin for infectious diseases and to develop it as a therapeutic agent.

The discoverer of a correlation may consider it trifling and far from the crucial regularities important for causal explanations in the problem area of his interest. Undoubtedly many of the correlations thus far discovered in the psychoanalytic situation are trivial. In depressing fact, our established regularities are few and loosely stated and our causal explanations are still too global for precise prediction and modification of behavior. Our thematic correlations differ from the propositional assertions idealized in physics in their openness, incompleteness, and explanation mainly by colligation. But we have a good first approximation and we should continue to search diligently for the necessary regularities. For not only does the psychoanalytic situation provide a unique type of private experience which can be described out loud to another person without penalty, but it also has created a new opportunity for a science of persons. There are two kinds of observation and confirmation in human experience which are fundamentally different. One relates to the self and the other to an external world. The observations and confirmations that we are most sure of concern our own inner experience. To make this private data public they must be described as testimony to another person. They become a part of science when recurring features are discovered in these inclusive self-descriptions and explanatory principles are formulated to account for them. Thus psychoanalysis bridges what is privately felt as true with what can be publicly demonstrated as true.

NOTES

1. The fable is a variation on a theme proposed by S. E. Perry, "Observations on Social Processes in Psychiatric Research," *Behavioral Science,* 1 (1956), 290-302.

2. S. Freud, "Contributions to the Psychology of Love. A Special Type of Choice of Object Made by Men," *Collected Papers* (New York: Basic Books, 1959), Vol. IV, pp. 192-202.

3. E. Nagel, "Principles of the Theory of Probability," in the *International Encyclopedia of Unified Science,* O. Neurath *et al.* [Eds.] (Chicago: University of Chicago Press, 1955), Vol. I, Part 2, pp. 341-422.

4. For a lucid account of the neoclassical position in probability theory, see I. J. Good, "Kinds of Probability," *Science,* 129 (1959), 443-447.

5. Every investigator in psychoanalysis should own, study, and restudy S. Siegel, *Non-parametric Statistics for the Behavioral Sciences* (New York: McGraw-Hill Book Co., 1956).

6. K. M. Colby, "Experiment on the Effects of an Observer's Presence on the Imago System During Psychoanalytic Free-Association," *Behavioral Science,* 5 (1960), 216-232.

7. The difficult problem of random samples in psychological and psychiatric research is compactly summarized in H. P. Iker, "Some Theoretical and Practical Aspects of Sampling Procedures in Research," *Journal of Nervous and Mental Disease,* 128 (1959), 191-203.

Conclusion

S CIENTIFIC INQUIRY begins with a problem and bright-idea hypotheses about it. To see a problem, to feel it is worth solving, and to search, guided by hypotheses, for the hidden explanatory pattern constitutes the essence of discovery. Those procedural rules which we term "scientific methods" do not create discoveries; they can only increase the probability that a discovery is true.

The solution of problems in psychoanalysis requires clinical experience to generate hypotheses and the use of appropriate scientific methods to indicate which of the hypotheses are empirically justified. Unless we are to paddle about in stagnant taxonomy, we must derive new hypotheses, press a search for the relevant facts of crucial regularities, measure those facts, and formulate their explanatory principles. These principles will be lawlike statements regarding the order and connectedness of events in person behavior. They will include statements about the priority of meanings and purposes which have coherence and internal consistency sufficient for causal explanation.

Psychoanalytic research intends to contribute to a science of persons. It is obvious that persons effect other persons in everyday life and it is striking how these effects are intensified in the psychoanalytic situation. If we can discover the patterns of such effects and isolate and refine the variables responsible, we should be able to increase our control over them. Such a search will be long, frustrating, and often defeating. But the frontier of science is like an art in that we make it up as we go along. This can be fun as well as toil, something investigators like to keep to themselves.

Index

Index

class, and generalization, 5, 74, 96 *ff.*, 106
clinical analytic situation, 26 *ff.*, 82 *ff.*
cognitive dissonance, 61
Colby, K. M., 108
collaboration, in analytic situation, 84-85
colligation, in explanation, 42
communication, in analytic situation, 85
communication theory, 62-63
computer programing, 37-38
concomitant variation, 37
confirmation
  of hypotheses, 7
  by self-observation, 87
conflict, 60, 61, 68
  pathogenic, 70
contingency coefficient, 99
controlling, of observation, 30 *ff.*
Copernicus, 11, 58
correlation
  in analytic situation, 89 *ff.*
  coefficient, 100
  erroneous, 91
  observational, 90-91
  Pearson product-moment, 100
  recurrent, 92 *ff.*
critique of psychoanalysis, 53 *ff.*
crucial regularities, 104 *ff.*

Dantzig, T., 23
Darwin, C., 30, 53, 73
decoding of messages, 34-35, 63
deductive method, 8, 18

defenses, 69-70
definition
  of psychoanalytic research, 83
  in science, 19
  of scientist, 5-7
Dement, W., 59, 76
description
  scientific, 34
  of self-observation, 83, 85, 89
discovery, in science, 109
domain
  of organisms, 58
  of persons, 13, 58, 86 *ff.*
  of things, 58, 86
dreams, 69
drive, 24, 60, 68
dynamics, 68

Einstein, A., 6, 18, 23
Ellis, A. E., 76
empathy, 83
empiricism, and rationalism, 8-11
energy, construct of cathexis, 67-68
error, Types I and II, 101
ethology, 59-60
Euclid, 9
evidence, weight of, 7, 95
experiment, 35 *ff.*
  of nature, 36
  planned, 36 *ff.*
explanation, 41-43
  causal, 107
  by colligation, 42
  definition of, 41

Index

explanation, and prediction, 43
Eysenck, J., 22

fallacy, of affirming consequent, 41-42
Feigl, H., 22, 59, 76
Fermat, P. de, 94
Festinger, L., 61, 77
Fleming, Sir A., 106
Fletcher, R., 61, 77
Florey, Sir H. W., 107
free association, 71
frequentist view of probability theory, 95
Freud, S., 28, 29, 51, 58, 62, 65-66, 73, 76, 77, 89, 90, 91, 108
functioning
  healthy, 67 *ff.*, 69
  pathologic, 69-70

Galileo, 11, 12
generalization, 5, 9, 13, 42, 74, 106
genes, and phylogenetic memories, 74
genetic process, in psychoanalytic theory, 68-69
Gerard, R., 59, 76
Goedel, K., 18, 23
Good, I. J., 108
Gordon, A., 45
Group for the Advancement of Psychiatry, 51

Hall, C., 61, 62, 76
Harvey, W., 14

healthy functioning, 67 *ff.*, 69
Heider, F., 61, 77
Helmholtz, H. von, 73
history
  and science, 74
  of science, 7 *ff.*
Holmes, O. W., 45
hypothesis
  null, 98 *ff.*
  selecting, 30

Iker, H. P., 108
inborn sets, and instinctual drive, 68
incest taboo, 62
inductive method, 17-18
information, definition of, 63
information theory
  mathematical, 63-64
  psychoanalytic, 63-64
innate patterns, and ethology, 60
input
  by analyst, 71-72
  variable in experiment, 37
integrative scale, in science, 57 *ff.*
interpretation, in psychoanalytic situation, 71-72
interval scale of measurement, 100
intervention, in psychoanalytic treatment, 71
introspection, 56, 83, 88

Kepler, J., 11
Kleitman, N., 76
Kluckhohn, C., 62, 77

Index

Index

observation, scientific, 24 *ff.*
  systematizing of, 26-28
observer
  independent, 31
  and observed in persons, 86-88
Occam, William of, 20
oral impregnation belief, 96 *ff.*
ordinal scale, in measurement,
    100
output variable in experiment, 37

parametric tests, 100
Pascal, B., 94
Pasteur, L., 58
pathology, psychoanalytic, 69-70
Perry, S. E., 108
persons
  in analytic situation, 84
  domain of, 13, 58, 86 *ff.*
  observation of, 86 *ff.*
  science of, 107
phylogenetic memories, 74-75
physics
  and procedural model, 13
  and scientific revolution, 11-14
Plato, and rationalism, 9
population, and sample, 33, 96,
    103-104
prediction and explanation, 42-43
principle, explanatory, 41-43
probability
  causal laws of, 93-94
  as degree of confirmation, 95-
    96
  as relative frequency, 94-95
  theory, 93 *ff.*

probability, use of, in psycho-
    analysis, 16, 17, 93 *ff.*
problem, role of, in science, 6
programing, of computers, 37-38
pseudo-explanation, 42-43
pseudo-problems, 19
  in psychoanalysis, 72-73
psychic apparatus, 24
psychoanalysis, criticism of as sci-
    ence, 4, 53 *ff.*
psychoanalyst, 84
  and research, 79 *ff.*
psychoanalytic situation
  description of, 84-85
  research in, 79 *ff.*
psychology, 61
  psychoanalytic, 67-69
psychopathology
  psychoanalytic, 69-70
psychoses, and psychoanalytic
    theory, 70
Pythagoras, 8

quantitation, 15
questions
  decidable in psychoanalysis, 6
  role of, in science, 6
  undecidable in psychoanalysis,
    73-74

random factors, 98
randomness, and probability, 103-
    104
ratio scale of measurement, 100
rationalism and empiricism, 8-11

Index